MEDICAL GROWING

A GARDEN OF PEACE

Written and Photographed by
By Daniel P. Boughen
Foreword by Ted Smith

Medical Growing – A Garden of Peace

Photo Art by Van M. Bigelow

Published by:
Trine Day LLC
PO Box 577
Walterville, OR 97489
1-800-556-2012
www.TrineDay.com
publisher@trineday.net

Library of Congress Control Number:
2018940780

Boughen, Daniel P.
Medical Growing: A Garden of Peace—2nd ed.
p. cm.
Includes bibliography.
Epub (ISBN-13) 978-1-63424-103-8
Kindle (ISBN-13) 978-1-63424-104-5
Print (ISBN-13) 978-1-63424-102-1
1. Cannabis. 2. Marijuana. 3. Cannabis – Growth 4. Cannabis – Handbooks, manuals, etc. 5. Marijuana – Handbooks, manuals, etc. 6. Cannabis – Propagation . 7. Marijuana – Propagation I. Title

Second Edition
10 9 8 7 6 5 4 3 2 1

Printed in Korea
Distribution to the Trade by:
Independent Publishers Group (IPG)
814 North Franklin Street
Chicago, Illinois 60610
312.337.0747
www.ipgbook.com

I dedicate this book to those persecuted and incarcerated by the War on Drugs, to my Father, who was organic before there was a movement, to Mum, who told me to "Write what I know," and to my love, Penny.

"One has a Moral Responsibility to disobey unjust Laws."
— Dr. Martin Luther King

This handbook will take you straight to the finished product in the shortest possible time with less power and effort, yielding healthier, happier plants, productive crops, and the best Cannabis you ever had! I hope you enjoy it.
Daniel Boughen

XXII, 5. 43. Cannabinaceae.

182. Cannabis sativa L. Hanf.

Table of Contents

FOREWORD

As the heavy veil of prohibition is lifted off the cannabis plant around the world, the incredible potential of the plant is being realized by those working close to it. Though science has made some significant advancement in our understanding of cannabis, it is clear many discoveries are yet to be made when it is no longer illegal to study or grow. By sharing knowledge of the medical and industrial uses of cannabis gained under the restraints of prohibition, pioneers like Daniel are setting the stage for a new era of terpene delight.

Although cannabis has been used for thousands of years, the prohibition of cannabis throughout most of the world in the last 100 years has effectively suppressed research into growing methods and medical uses. Over the last 4 decades, enthusiasts in North America have defied the law and grown cannabis, first outdoors and gradually moving into greenhouses, basements, sheds and bunkers. While many books have been written about growing, many secrets about the plant have not yet been revealed.

Growing your own medicine and food has many benefits that should not be underestimated. Engaging with nature is becoming more difficult for those living in urban settings. The sense of well-being one can feel when surrounded by big, healthy cannabis plants is invigorating, especially for those suffering from anxiety, PTSD and even pain. Moreover, growing your own cannabis is important for those of us who love the herb and could never afford to purchase all they wish to consume, even if it was available in legal market. Even though the cost of purchasing cannabis is likely to drop when it becomes legal, it will still be far above costs of production and for those ready, willing and able to grow there should be nothing stopping us. Growing your own medicine will not only make sure you have an inexpensive source of high-quality medicine, but it will help keep the prices down on the market as the industry must keep the prices low enough that there is not a great incentive to grow your own.

Ultimately there should be greenhouses growing cannabis for food, medicine and fuel in every senior center, hospital and school. As the fear of cannabis subsides, these institutions will learn to embrace to various uses of cannabis, incorporating the herb into the daily lives of patients, elderly and students alike.

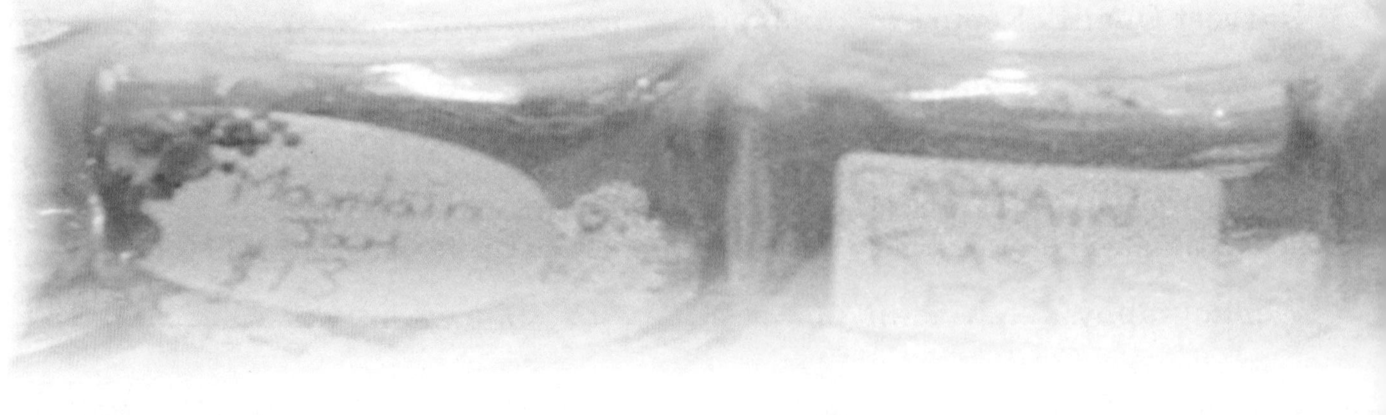

From the beginning of life to the end, cannabis should become our primary source of health and vitality. As the trend of growing food and herb gardens in urban settings builds, so to will the interest in growing cannabis. Since a greenhouse makes the most sense for growing cannabis, there will no doubt be a surge of new structures put up when it becomes legal to grow a personal garden. Many used urban spaces should be filled with greenhouses growing cannabis and other agricultural products for local consumption. Small, self-contained indoor gardens will become common as good medicine and food become more expensive, if it is available at all.

In a time when most people living in urban centers are losing touch with nature, growing your own food and medicine could not be more important.

Simply watching a seed sprout and grow into a fully mature plant can be rewarding, especially for people with mental or physical disabilities. Encouraging the elderly and disabled to grow cannabis gives them an opportunity to enjoy the vibrant energy that a room full of plants emits.

However, there is a very real threat that the end of prohibition could turn into a corporate bonanza if citizens are forced to purchase cannabis from companies rather than being given the option of growing themselves. While there are no doubt regulations and taxes should be applied to anything sold to the public, it is also logical to assume individuals should have the power to provide for themselves if possible. However, keeping it illegal to grow your own cannabis is what governments in countries like Canada are trying to do, creating a rich market for large companies at the expense of patients who could otherwise provide for themselves.

That is why it is important for every grower to educate themselves and others about the benefits of cannabis and the problems with prohibition. While that is difficult for many to do, as the fear created by prohibition still causes many to remain silent for the sake of their family, there are still many ways people in the cannabis industry can help free the weed. Every opportunity to gently inform family, friends, neighbors, coworkers, government officials or strangers about the wondrous gifts of the herb need to be taken. For, as this book is being published we are in very critical times.

The foundations for the future cannabis industry are being laid. It is very important that citizens have the option of growing their own plants and making extractions from it, or purchase what they desire from properly regulated commercial operations. Whether the new regime will work in everyone's best interest will in large part depend upon the general sentiment of the public, which will rely heavily on what the average person knows about cannabis.

Whether it is by supporting important court cases, making art with pot leaves on it, writing letters to the press, growing plants, reading cannabis history books, commenting on social media, passing out cannabis literature on the bus or bringing up the subject to your sick aunt at the family gathering, if cannabis has helped you then you owe it. Few causes in life will give you the satisfaction that you can receive from working with the cannabis plant. Let your imagination flow and you will find you can do something you love that will also help contribute to a better future for the cannabis plant.

The people openly working in the field tend to be among the most kind-hearted, open and generous souls you could hope to meet. The plant itself just gives and gives. For those willing to do the work and take the risk, entering the cannabis field at this point in history is exciting, interesting and fulfilling.

Kudos to Daniel for giving so much. His reward is your harvest.

Ted Smith

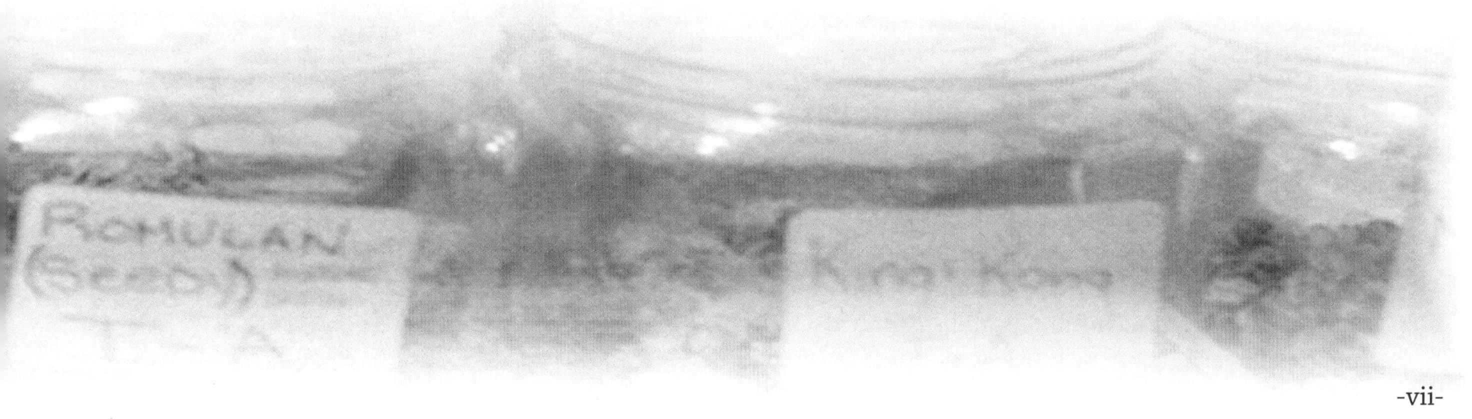

INTRODUCTION

Cannabis will soon be legal nationally. The bigoted treatment and moral wrongs being committed against Cannabis smokers must come to an end in the name of our civil and constitutional rights, our health and environment, and for our peace and humanity. Cannabis prohibition laws are now under attack, and the rest of the world watches as citizens who are now better educated than ever about side effects, drugs and addiction decide for themselves that Cannabis is safe in spite of decades of state propaganda.

With legalization, the production, distribution and regulation of Cannabis could be taken out of the hands of organized crime, where poor product quality and the presence of impurities, violence and association with hard drugs presently makes purchasing Cannabis dangerous. Cannabis must be put back under the control of the people who need and enjoy it.

The billions that the sale of Cannabis generates on the black market could instead pay unionized workers in a legal industry, where the funds will be contributing to local economies and federal social welfare instead of propping up organized crime networks. It would instead support our communities.

We need the unity within the Cannabis community to expand to the general public, and so we must keep providing proper information and publicly calling a bad policy what it is. We must mobilize human rights groups to once again overturn unfair prohibition laws in our respective countries. This is an international human rights issue and deserves to be treated as such. To grow Cannabis for your personal medicine is now an act of patriotism.

The world's citizens have been the victims of a huge corporate scam. Clearly, those corporations that demanded and received 'natural human rights' have abused them, and killed millions of law-abiding citizens, even above and beyond the drug war. As citizens, they have proven to be criminals, who rape resources and cause environmental disasters, attempting to subvert democracy at every turn; acts that would land any real human citizen in prison. As bad citizens, corporations must necessarily bear responsibility for their acts, and in some cases must be brought to account and suffer the legal consequences for crimes against humanity, namely corporate death.

Its shocking to note that the same corporations that presently destroy the environment and rape the resources under government license support the prohibition of hemp and Cannabis, and lobby against legalization. It is important that those corporate rights be dissolved, so that greedy corporate shareholders creating the inflated false economy no longer control the reins of government. Write now, and demand that your local, county, state, provincial and federal representatives hear that human rights are for humans, and we want them. Corporate rights are simply laughable. Money has no rights at all.

A Little About Myself

As the son of a nurseryman, I suppose I have some instincts when it comes to plants, but the last thing I will claim is that I am some all-knowing master grower. Often my curiosity takes me down a rabbit hole, and I live to make startling discoveries which blow the lid off conventional wisdom. It is akin to finding a precious jewel in the rubbish heap.

I call on my observation of nature to help me understand what is going on during the course of my grows, and asking myself what normally happens in the great outdoors has always helped to guide me in the right direction, and look for clues in nature to the right ways of living from the surrounding world. More often than not, the simple solution nature offers is superior to anything on the shelf.

I first started studying the commercial aspects of hemp back in 1998, and soon realized that the importance of Cannabis went far beyond its enjoyment, with the potential to provide a strong world ecology and economy, and even clean up the toxic oil mess plaguing the world today. My interest in Cannabis was soon stimulated by the very amazing history of our former world-wide hemp economy, which helped fuel the coming of the age of reason, not to mention the rapid growth and expansion of the British Empire.

My original guide was posted online in 1998. In it I provided information about common growing practices after discovering that members in Cannabis forums at the time were as likely to provide bad data as good information, and real expertise was difficult to find due to the secretive and proprietary nature of the practice. It was a very basic guide, but it helped many find instruction and reliable assistance on the basics of growing without wasting time on misinformation.

Eventually a forum was erected, and a Compassionate Community was established where kindness was the rule, and soon honest and helpful members gathered and provided new growers with good information in a non-judgmental, honest and helpful learning environment. The forum and community at howsitgoineh.com is still there, and continues to inspire the content of this book.

If you have an interest in the many properties of Cannabis and hemp, I encourage you to seek out all the information you can, but be prepared to wade through an incredible volume of information, and to have an open mind about what Cannabis is and where its real potential lies. You may find your head spinning as you learn the truth. I was once told that one could spend his entire life studying, and never successfully know everything there is to know about roses, a plant family cultivated since before the days of Rome, and having thousands of cultivars and subspecies, including apples.

Likewise, the true wonders of Cannabis as yet remain undiscovered, but the amount of new information out there now is overwhelming, with more discoveries coming daily on the internet. Websites have become the engine for social change and the dissemination of free information about Cannabis. All we need to do is go with an open mind and look!

I hope that for the sake of your health you will study and grow your own Cannabis.

Peace,

Daniel P Boughen

Cannabis is Good For You!

I am about to make the argument that Cannabis is in fact health food, in that its overall effect on the nervous system is one of beneficial easement, while at the same time it is the least toxic natural herbal substance known to man.

Toxic experimental drugs cause incredible damage. The use of Cannabis can replace many of the pharmaceutical drugs being used today. We still wait in vain for science's unfulfilled promise of the true Cancer cure. Pharmaceuticals have failed to copy what Cannabis has done for thousands of years.

Studies have shown that Cannabis protects the brain, regulates the nervous system, attacks and kills cancer cells, and eases dozens of other aches and pains.

Here are just a few of the afflictions Cannabis safely provides regular symptomatic relief from:

- **Chronic pain from arthritis**
- **Joint Inflammation**
- **Pain from repetitive workplace injury**
- **Recovery from alcoholism or narcotics**
- **Menstrual symptoms**
- **Wasting diseases related to HIV**
- **Nausea due to Chemotherapy**
- **Fatigue**
- **Migraines**
- **Fibromyalgia**
- **Chrohn's disease**
- **Multiple Sclerosis**
- **Erectile Dysfunction**
- **Cancer**

While there may be useful drugs that can help to manage some of the symptoms brought on by these diseases *(many by accident)*, their toxicity and addictive nature remain a serious concern for patients. Their inability to cure disease is not in question, since they do not. Curing disease is not the aim of pharmaceutical companies, they aim much lower at the highly lucrative symptom management market. Frankly, to the CEO's of pharmaceutical companies it makes more business sense to *never* cure a disease.

Experimental chemicals designed to treat the many and varied and even imaginary illnesses of humans carry with them the additional risk of creating complications, which may require further treatment with other pharmaceutical drugs.

Patients who are forced into a vulnerable position can be drawn in to an increasingly addictive drug spiral. They can easily end up socially unable to cope and hopelessly addicted to opiates prescribed by their doctors. Families are destroyed by the increasing incidence of accidental overdose of patients on prescription drugs.

When you consider that the Endo-Cannabinoid system has already been present in our bodies for countless eons, a new respect for herbal medicine can be properly appreciated.

Cannabis remains the only herbal medicine able to regulate such a wide array of systems in the body, while providing a non-toxic and non-addictive relaxant. Sociologically, the lasting presence of debate about Cannabis serves to strongly indicate that prohibition is no longer appropriate, and that an educated public doesn't agree with the DEA's status for Cannabis.

Now professors, doctors, scientists and health professionals of the highest integrity are finally able to confirm what we have known all along, and help debunk the ridiculous gateway theory and other vain prohibitionist propaganda. The tenor of the debate has risen. Even health and legal professionals with law enforcement are speaking out against racist drug policy, acknowledging Cannabis's safety and supporting broad legalization.

Reports from patients are empirical; they use Cannabis for pain relief, and it works. Such overwhelming evidence has come to light that no one may ever say it is useless again.

It has now become our moral duty to perform an act of civil disobedience, and grow it in protest of the arbitrary and racist laws prohibiting it. If that sounded familiar it should. Dr. Martin Luther King once spoke similar words in support of civil rights for all Americans. Cannabis prohibition is a civil rights issue too, and the thin edge of the wedge. If Cannabis user's rights can be overridden, then none of us is safe from the whims of the state. Your other rights could easily be next.

Cannabis is Not Toxic!

As a safe recreational substance, Cannabis has no equal. Its gentle resins stimulate our Endocannabinoid system, releasing the dopamine we produce in our brains and providing an all-natural relaxation that is absolutely supreme in peace and joy.

Cannabis leaves nothing in the way of hangovers like alcohol. It is nontoxic, and proven non-addictive. Cannabis stimulates creativity, serenity, and well being, inhibits ego, promotes friendliness and peaceful cooperation. Its mildly euphoric effects are easy to dismiss, and 20 to 50 million Americans use it with no ill side effects whatsoever.

Cannabis users are not prone to fighting, foolish, dangerous behavior or violence. Opting instead for cooperation, we are apt to eat fine food, listen to good music, dance with our loved ones, and care for our families, grow a garden, paint a masterpiece, or even draft a constitution!

Family dysfunction and violence that is caused by alcoholism is nonexistent in Cannabis smokers. In fact Cannabis's relaxant properties have proven an effective remedy for addictions, such as tobacco, alcohol, cocaine, and heroin, and show promise with methamphetamine addiction as well.

Cannabis shows promise as a social remedy to harder drugs, offering a safe alternative for those who wish to alter their collective consciousness, and for whom alcohol is not a viable choice.

To be clear, in five thousand years of documentation on the medical and recreational use of Cannabis, there has never been recorded a single death directly caused by Cannabis toxicity.

In strictest medical terms, Cannabis is the safest food on the planet, with an LD50 rating so ridiculously low they can only estimate its numbers.

LD50 for Cannabis is estimated at 1:40,000

Consider this in real terms. It means that in order to induce a lethal dose, the subject would need to consume such a ***ridiculously*** large *(22 to 45 pounds)* amount of Cannabis in a single sitting that its sheer impossibility renders the study's application to Cannabis invalid. Long before the subject reached his goal, he would be overcome with $C0_2$ or carbon monoxide asphyxiation.

So, clearly Cannabis can kill you if a 50 pound bale falls on your head, or if you are killed by Carbon monoxide poisoning from a burning bale, but smoking Cannabis even daily won't come even close to risking your health, and may in fact improve it. Feel free to mock the invalid application of the LD50 rating to Cannabis; it's being misused.

Obviously, toxicity is the wrong criterion by which to measure Cannabis. The focus of medical study needs to be shifted, and standards of cell, nervous system and endocrine health need to be applied and Cannabis must be given the same due diligence as the LD50 toxicity ratings.

Studies of Cannabis should focus on the benefits of its use on the health of the subject as a target for information gathering. Science in the field of Cannabis has a long road ahead, and the medical community needs to bring focused attention to bear, and make certain it is properly studied to see the real benefits.

Asking what is nutritious about Cannabis may be a more constructive approach to learning. Perhaps this could also be applied as an equal and opposite balancing study to more natural foods and drugs. As it is, the LD50 rating system is only useful as far as its bias allows, and so has a limited application to the expression of balanced scientific research.

At this point, we may confidently and empirically say it is not dangerous. Asking what is toxic about Cannabis is just disingenuous.

The LD50 for Cannabis is a crock! Created in 1927 by J.W. Trevan, the LD50 rating is used by science to determine the toxicity of substances. Every drug is given this rating, and Cannabis is no exception and yet, to date, no one has been able to accurately determine Cannabis's lethal dosage.

What Cannabis Will Replace

Stock held corporations have been the eternal buzz-kill since time began. Charles Dickens's dire warning about corporate slavery in *A Christmas Carol,* and the notorious and omnipotent Big Brother of *1984* by George Orwell featured chilling examples of corporate control gone amuck. Even in the new media, stories like this still serve as warnings about the dark potential of so-called *'corporate culture'*; a term cooked up by corporate public relations in a pathetic attempt to sanitize greed. Lets face it, business is all about profit. You buy something, and you sell it for more. There is no humanity in an entity whose programmed purpose is to make money for its shareholders to the exclusion of every other consideration. Any such corporation is soulless and undeserving of existence.

What else has the government lied about?

When government (whose sworn interest is to protect the people) acts like a private company or presumes to take on a pseudo-corporate role, and joins in collusion with the interests of corporations and money, there is an inherent social conflict of interest since the people who elected their representatives can no longer trust them.

Many politicians, agencies and corporations lined up to lie about Cannabis and rape the economy. They not only shut down the hemp industry and took over medicine with chemicals, but they also systematically raped the environment for profit in housing, fiber, and energy instead of using environmentally friendly Cannabis.

This monumental corporate greed culminated in April 20, 2010 with the British Petroleum spill in the Gulf of Mexico, but let's not forget the remaining environment worldwide. Whole areas are now uninhabitable, millions are in prison, and obedient prescription junkies walk the earth, blindly doing as they are told. The government has used drug enforcement agencies and the people's free press to slander Cannabis with bald-face lies and *racisim,* to attack a far superior product and gain market advantage for petroleum and pharmaceutical companies. they are poisoning our bodies and our world.

Moguls like William Randolph Hearst and Dupont wished to dominate the market and fiber industries with their petroleum-based chemicals and timber products, so they lied to the world. They employed social terrorism in their phony articles about 'reefer madness', and targeted the weakest and most vulnerable members of society with yellow journalism so they could appear to be protecting public morals, while the government of the day passed oppressive or unconstitutional laws designed to limit citizen's freedoms and choices and consolidate power.

All along the way, this corruption has controlled the media and used it to confuse the public with propaganda campaigns run on television, on the one hand touting experimental drugs and better living for all through chemical science, while on the other supporting a pseudo-moral call for an imaginary 'drug free society'.

They've succeeded only in polluting and destroying land, air and sea, and destroying lives with human experiments, all in the name of progress – but progress may go backwards when there is talk of the EPA being defunded. Cannabis can replace all of that, and I and all those who write after me can prove it.

You Can't spell 'Pharmaceuticals without 'harm'

In the late 1950s and early 1960s, more than 10,000 children in 46 countries were born with serious deformities such as phocomelia, as a consequence of ***thalidomide*** use as a seditive. (ref. Wikipedia)

Cannabis Therapy

Cannabis has been used for centuries for symptomatic relief from cocaine and heroin addiction, even before the arrival of powerful mu-opioids anti-psychotics and mood enhancing pharmaceuticals which now flood society. Many of the most popularly used and vigorously advertised pharmaceutical drugs come with a sharply addictive profile and a long list of side effects. Once prescribed patients may be on them for years or even the rest of their lives.

This often puts people's health in decline as the side effects of years of use accumulate, weakening the body's systems and eventually shutting down the Endo-Cannabinoid system.

Cannabis may be used to ease withdrawal pains during a patient's convalescence. When combined with practical advice and peer counseling, Cannabis provides a safe and non-toxic alternative to addiction relapse, and has the potential to be more successful than the traditional 'cold turkey' treatment programs.

Recreational drugs can also cause addiction, the most common being alcohol, and illegal drugs such as heroin, methamphetamines or crack cocaine, but so can prescription drugs.

With alcohol, constant low-level poisoning affects self esteem, suppresses the natural immune system, and its use is highly addictive. Without the means to 'chemically decompress', the person trying to break his addiction may easily suffer relapse.

A simple Cannabis treatment for severe addiction from opiates or other medications may take as little as four weeks, starting with oils or tinctures for the severest symptoms, and symptomatically selected buds for relaxation and mood enhancement through a patient's initial decompression period.

Legal acceptance of Cannabis as medicine will go a long way towards offering people in trouble a means to win. Once a person has declared his desire to end his addiction it is our duty as his fellows to assist his efforts, and respectfully facilitate an exit strategy for him. Cannabis is one of the best.

Addiction counseling could be offered on a voluntary base or if needed, in combination with psychological counseling and guidance.

In our own hands

The simple knowledge of the healing power of Cannabis puts control back in peoples hands. We are now acutely aware of the danger and power of addictions, and the negative effects they may have on our lives.

The friends we have lost wait for us to share this information, and many long to use Cannabis to help them back from the dangerous world of hard drugs and highly addictive substances.

Recovery from an addiction is a difficult journey. Patients suffer psychological as well as a chemical imbalance in the body. Addictive substances such as heroin, alcohol or prescription drugs directly cause the suppression of the Endocannabinoid system present in our bodies, and in order to restore health, the dormant Cannabinoid receptors need to be reactivated.

A patient may need a highly potent dose using oils or tinctures at the beginning of treatment to reawaken these receptors so they may work to reinforce the immune system and restore the body balance. The psychoactive and relaxant qualities of Cannabis initially allow the patient to rest, help control craving and prevent relapses.

The 'Munchie Effect' Cannabis produces encourages the patient to begin eating, so gradually, vitality can be returned to the body as protein, minerals and vitamins are returned to normal levels.

Once the initial 'decompression period' has been concluded, the patient ceases oils and tinctures in favor of the appropriate titration of vaporized or smoked Cannabis, reinforcing the patients ability to avoid relapse.

Drug rehabilitation is an ongoing process which may take years to accomplish. Although Cannabis is not addictive, long established addictive habits may be difficult to break, and former addicts may opt to use Cannabis the rest of their lives. Still, this constitutes legitimate medical use, and not drug abuse. In the context of balancing the Endocannabinoid system there can be no abuse of Cannabis whatsoever.

Why You Should Grow Cannbis For Your Personal Health

The three-letter government agencies have made us all the chattel of vast corporate conglomerates, which devour resources and churn out endless piles of crap for us to consume; and we, the willing participants, run until we die like a hamster on a wheel.

Our role in this dark and macabre production is to work at social slavery jobs for money to purchase the crap that the corporations sell us, thereby completing the circle of consumption. They bribe us with bright and shiny consumer goods to keep us quiet, so they may go on raping the world for money and power with our cooperation.

Without your help buying products and validating the corporate bottom line, they cannot exist, and using Cannabis instead of pharmaceuticals or as a social relaxant is a serious financial attack on those corporate profits.

Oh, they will loudly cry foul. They will say that if Cannabis is legalized all kinds of terrible consequences will ensue, *(actually their likely demise)* and immediately roll out more of their terrorist propaganda, but, don't believe it anymore. Frankly, all their deceptions have already been exposed and exploded.

Right now corporate entities are attempting to take over and control the Cannabis industry in a pitiful attempt to continue their corrupt model of unfettered avarice.

Pharmaceutical companies earn five times the profit margin of other Fortune-500 companies.

Consequences may be dire for the profits of "Big Pharma" if Cannabis is legalized outright, but it is those very earnings which leave a wake of addiction and social destruction. We may even thank the industry for presenting a version of corporate greed so evil that it becomes obvious that policies and laws must be changed.

What is good for the pharmaceutical industry is absolutely and unequivocally *not* what is good for the rest of the world. It is corporate greed that is the enemy of the people, and it is corporations who are the real terrorists.

The concentration of money lets people die who might have lived for lack of care, it steals and never gives back, it is a black hole from which nothing returns. Big Pharma is the poster child for greed.

We are declaring a war too, on greed. We can implement the War on Greed with peaceful gardening of the Cannabis plant.

When you grow your own Cannabis, cure your own ailments, and feed yourself, you will free yourself from the corporate rat-race, so they may no longer steal from you or put you on the prescription drug mill. Here is the real irony: Cannabis will help you live drug free!

EPA: Without the *Environmental Protection Agency* forcing corporations to adopt environmentally friendly practices they would have continued polluting like spoiled children, since corporations have absolutely NO self-control when it comes to environmental rape in search of easy profit).

Legalization Models and Society

The corporate model

Monopolistic models for the corporatization of Cannabis are now being presented by lobby groups who want to cash in on Cannabis in order to sustain the inflated profits of Big Pharma. They fully expect to continue to charge the same 'street prices' in the new market; however, such expectations are highly unrealistic, since it was prohibition that caused the price of Cannabis to sky-rocket.

Seventy plus years of prohibition has raised the value of Cannabis to ten times its natural market value due to the risk and danger posed by law enforcement when one is involved in its production and distribution!

If we know anything about how markets work, we are aware that normal production in a free market will cause prices to drop as market saturation is reached, and new companies with improved products enter the market. Consumers will 'vote with dollars' as they always have, and the company best able to anticipate will prevail in their local market.

A monopoly on Cannabis by the government would completely control production. Under this law only licensed corporations would be allowed to cultivate, breed and provide Cannabis, corporate patents would control all Cannabis strains and allow legal action against citizens. Licensed seed companies would then limit the selection, dilute potency, insert 'terminator genes' so plants can't be seeded, and then deliberately jack up the price to maximize profit.

To preserve the biodiversity of the species, our access to specific strains grown for taste or symptoms, the people must remain the custodians of Cannabis, and keep it in the public domain. Recent efforts to patent strains should be resisted; it's just another attempt by corporations to rob us of our natural rights.

Another legalization model

In a more humane and so far unconsidered model, governments would give up their erroneous propaganda campaigns against Cannabis and concede defeat, thus ending the war of a government against its people, and leveling the playing field. Cannabis should be legal to possess, cultivate, buy, sell, process, ingest, share or study under a comprehensive, compassionate civil law based on the human rights enshrined in every constitution.

Cannabis seeds should be widely available, and the people should once again be guaranteed their personal rights to privacy. Our growth as humanity depends on being free from persecution or criminalization by law enforcement from a government with a corporate interest in the petroleum, plastic, pharmaceuticals and industrial prison complex.

Cannabis eradication programs should be scrapped, the DEA de-funded and dismantled, and all terrorism against Cannabis using citizens worldwide should cease. The corrupt enemies of liberty should be tried and imprisoned for their crimes against humanity. Real law enforcement would get a boost of billions to their budgets as funds are reallocated and resources redirected.

We could stop building prisons and shut down those that are no longer needed, and the non-violent Cannabis prisoners would no longer get training by the justice system in how to be better, smarter criminals. They could instead create music, art and literature for the good of society using Cannabis as their inspiration for peace and spiritual growth (as it has been for centuries).

With the end of corruption, the industrial hemp plant can be studied and grown widely to help improve our physical environment and build a new greener economy. Hemp products can mitigate our need for fossil fuels, growing hemp crops can reclaim poisoned lands and improve soil; an acre of Cannabis filters five times the $C0^2$ as an acre of forest, as it provides textiles, fiber, paper, medicines, fuel and many other products in a yearly crop that is sustainable.

Lying to the people may have served governments in the past, but the degradation of democracy can no longer stand. Their treason has been revealed, and they deserve to be put in the very prisons they built to pay for waging this immoral war against the people.

Government credibility is at an all-time low. It can only be re-established when the "public" servants, currently usurping our collective will and selling out our natural rights to corporate interests, are brought to justice.

Events unfolding across the Middle East indicate a growing awareness of the past foibles of human generations, and a determined willingness to bring about equity and social change, demonstrating that dictators may fall when measured by the masses. It is clear that with enough pressure our world can change, once human rights challenge corporate greed. It's true, terminally ill patients need Cannabis the most, but normal people sickened by Big Pharma need it also.

Let growing Cannabis become a symbol for freedom.

Cannabis and Its Place in Society

Are we setting a good example for our kids?

Some of the War on Drugs (WOD) campaigns ask the above question, but information about Cannabis presented through the media contains veiled moral judgments, legal threats, insinuations, pseudo-factoids, and outright lies. Our kids know this, and they can tell when we lie to them. It is an outrageous hypocrisy to tell children that Cannabis is dangerous while allowing alcohol usage. By supporting the lie, you risk your kids' trust and sow mistrust in your family. I myself recall this lie eroding my trust in my own parents, causing me all types of problems with trust issues later in life.

In fact, some of the most amazing, talented and successful people throughout history were Cannabis users. I'm certain you will recognize many of the names in the incomplete list to the right.

To this day Musicians, scholars, actors, artists, religious leaders, legal professionals, policemen, soldiers, and millions of other productive people use Cannabis responsibly without any negative consequences whatsoever – beyond the stigma of prohibition.

All of the arts have benefitted from the use of Cannabis. It doesn't cause aggressive behavior or possess toxic properties of other substances, and Cannabis is without the addictive profiles characterized by drugs such as tobacco, caffeine, alcohol, cocaine, methamphetamines or prescription opiates.

Cannabis stimulates thought, creativity, and peaceful cooperation, and many of the other qualities we find aesthetically desirable in human kind, and yet with Cannabis prohibition, these are not being stimulated in our society. When we prohibit Cannabis, we also prohibit our culture's artistic and creative growth.

So, what kind of message does Cannabis prohibition send to our kids? It says that anything can be done in the name of an unjust law, and that a corrupt and hypocritical administration thinks your rights are less important than their agenda. But when the world's children speak, do politicians listen?

It is a mistake to think that our children can't tell the difference between the truth and drug war propaganda. They know they are being lied to. In a few years our kids will be making the legalization of Cannabis a priority, since they also know that prohibition and corruption sets a bad example for their kids in the future. Tomorrow's parents know by first-hand experience that telling their children lies causes more harm in their families than Cannabis *ever* could.

Successful and historical tokers

George Washington
Thomas Jefferson
Benjamin Franklin
Barack Obama
George Washington Carver
Sir Winston Churchill
Bill Clinton
Dawn Wells
John Lennon
Ray Charles
Shen Nung
Robert Mitchum
Steve Martin
Walter Benjamin
Dr Lester Grinspoon
Johnny Depp
Timothy Leary
Peter Tosh
Bob Marley
Kate Moss
Art Garfunkel
Bob Denver
Burt Reynolds
Bruce Lee
Louis Armstrong
Bob Hope
Salvidor Dali
Steven King
Ted Turner
Tommy Chong
Jack Nicholson
Jennifer Aniston
Richard Pryor
Rodney Dangerfield
Oliver Stone
Jane Fonda
William Shakespeare
George Clooney
Margaret Mead
Michael Bloomberg
Macaulay Caulkin
Jack Layton
Peter Sellers
Oscar Wilde
Larry Hagman
Bing Crosby
Pablo Picasso
Woody Harrelson
Bill Gates
Pierre Elliot Trudeau
Dennis Hopper
Montel Williams
Eminem
Pancho Villa
Howard Marks
John Sinclair
Chrissie Hynde
George Harrison
Dizzy Gillespie
Snoop Dogg
Kareem Abdul-Jabbar
Hunter S. Thompson
Paul McCartney
Friedrich Nietzsche
Rudolf Nureyev
Richard Feynman
Thelonius Monk
Brad Pitt
Terence McKenna
Joe Pietri
Willie Nelson
Peter Fonda
Newt Gingrich
Sting
Milton Berle
Bill Murray
Bill Maher
Kirk Tousaw
Carl Sagan
Marc Emery
Ross Rebagliati
Sir Richard Branson
Queen Victoria
Jesus Christ

(Indeed, tokers have been influencing Art and culture for many millennia!)

A "12-1" Revolution

There is a new wave of thought now occurring about Cannabis, as growers begin to ask some of the right questions about growing conditions and the most effective way of achieving the best results from their medical grows. Unfortunately, good information on growing Cannabis has been hard to find, since much of the current information repeated ad nauseum on Cannabis is erroneous, having been warped by the misuse of a single factor of the growing process: lighting.

It seems obvious that the proper lighting cycle for Cannabis shouldn't be any different from any other short-day flowering plant here on planet earth, where global lighting never passes sixteen hours of daylight for the day and yet, for thirty years "Weed Gurus" have said that Cannabis needs eighteen hours of light to stay in a vegetative state. (Lighting schedules such as the "12-1" show that this isn't the case. "Sweat-shop" lighting won't give you a better yield, only tired plants.)

For Cannabis to have a8n eighteen hour day and a six hour night, it would have to have been created under unnatural planetary conditions. A planetary body being roughly a sphere can only be lit on one half of its surface, or twelve hours at a time by a single light source such as our sun. To cover more surface area and create an 18/6 cycle would require TWO light sources. I nearly went out of my mind trying to imagine the gravitational forces and planetary orbits for a model with twin stars. In fact, 18 hour lighting is so unnatural that few other plants on earth could possibly survive it, since such lighting conditions do not exist anywhere, and it does not fit in with the planets natural eco-sphere. It is a testament to Cannabis's toughness that it can stand so much abuse and still survive.

The authors who wrote that Cannabis should be grown under eighteen-hour conditions are simply mistaken, and yet one has to wonder why botanical experts ignored these falsehoods. One may postulate that the prohibitionist social atmosphere frowned on botanical experts either proving or disproving anything written about Cannabis. Still, their tacit support of an erroneous botanical principle allowed the creation of an entire industry that produces a highly stressed, tired out and weakened plant. Indeed, correct information on growing Cannabis and Hemp was available from historical references and current materials on growing other short-day plants applies.

Cannabis Sativa has been historically known as the easiest to grow, one of the most abundant plants on earth, yet bad information has made it more difficult to grow and more expensive, as well as indirectly blackmailing illegal growers who can't possibly complain about over-hyped and over-priced products. Further, while they somewhat recognize that Cannabis is a short-day plant, the "Gurus" incorrectly report that twelve hours is sufficient to properly flower Cannabis. Back here on earth, a short day is when the hours drop below eleven hours in the tropics or nine hours in northern climates. Again, a fundamentally mistaken hypothesis retards flowering because twelve hours light is neither short nor long, but intermediate length. This confuses the plant and actually prevents it from fully entering bloom.

These writers completely ignore over a century of research and work

on photo-periodic lighting by botanical specialists who discuss light interruption during night cycles to prevent short day plants from flowering.

Cannabis growers who formerly used 18/6 and 12/12 lighting have seen an improvement in plant health brought about by the 12-1 lighting. When they switched, they immediately noticed a difference in their crops and in their power bills, and have begun teaching 12-1 as well. We want everyone to know this information, in order to set growers free.

The work of the world-wide network of conscientious teachers has begun. These are growers with a moral credo like the hippy I once met, who asked as payment only that I teach others how to grow and pass on the wisdom and the positive karma of kindness.

There are now thousands of growers worldwide being taught the 12-1 method in spite of the reluctance of mainstream publishers to introduce it. The destruction of good information about Cannabis has been followed by a campaign of disinformation to undermine its use by making it as difficult to grow as possible.

A 12-1 "Army of Growers" is now well positioned from coast to coast in Canada, the US, Australia, Europe, and in countries all over the world. So that the misinformation and propaganda may be swept aside, we will continue to teach as many people as possible about the history, uses and cultivation of Cannabis.

Let no one forget how the War of Drugs has been waged, and how the conditions of prohibition allowed incorrect botanical techniques to be spread with no rebuttal from the botanical literati. Further, these artificially concocted methods required special nutrients from which sprang an entire industry of opportunistic quasi-scientists who broke apart formulae and sold them piece by piece at the greatest profit possible.

The 12-1 Army is online in peer to peer and patient group message boards and forums, sharing and writing until the mistakes made about Cannabis are corrected.

A 'DAY' IN THE LIFE OF CANNABIS

Cannabis falls in to the category of Short-Day Plants, and is governed by the same flowering rules flowers such as the African Marigold, and Poinsettia, which are commercially grown in the industry according to the guidelines set out for short-day plants.

Short-day plants must have a flowering period of less than eleven hours, or the plant remains partially in vegetation. Botanists have long since classified all plants including Cannabis according to their seasonal flowering behavior, and produced proven tables defining the length of seasons required for each genus to produce the optimum results. Their centuries of work archives results obtained from meticulously studying short-day, long-day and season-neutral flowering plants.

Recent evidence shows that twelve hour lighting is the cause of elongation of the branches and wider spacing of internode stems. Flowers and oils are underproduced, and vegetation continues, though at a decreased rate. The stored nutrients such as Nitrogen may not last long enough to sustain the flowering season, causing over or underfeeding complications.

Strong flowering is induced within only a few days of switching to Diminished Lighting, and is very often finished a week sooner than the strain information. Eight week strains may be finished in seven, ten week strains in only eight or nine weeks and so on. Diminished Lighting accelerates the flowering schedule considerably on all strains. Nutrients provided to the plants are used at a slower, steadier rate to more effectively produce oils, terpenes and medicinal compounds.

HOW WE CAN HELP CANNABIS

- **Talk about Cannabis to everyone.**

Cannabis can replace over 50,000 products we use every day. The name 'Cannabis' means easily grown — it asks for little, needs no pesticides, and repairs the land. It is a well- documented plant, used by mankind since the dawn of civilization. Hemp/Cannabis has the capability to fix much of the damage by big oil and big pharma.

- **Research all information for accuracy.**

Be curious, and do the work to find your own information on gardening. Google terms such as photoperiodism, diminished lighting, short and long day plants, and learn about the history and use of Cannabis/Hemp. EDUCATE yourself.

- **Protect and preserve pure genetic phenotypes.**

Make and save seeds from pure strains, and share them with friends and family. The posterity of Cannabis can be reserved by the people, for the people.

- **Observe and respond, learn the plant's language.**

Only make one change at a time, and observe for a week to see results, especially when still learning how the plants react. If you make several changes at once, you won't be able to ascertain results.

- **Cooperate with the plant's biology.**

Instead of forcing it to grow with over-lighting with massive doses of fertilizer that linger in the plant and leave unpleasant flavors, consider the plant's needs and health and light and feed accordingly. Trusting that the plant knows what it is doing is key to growing top shelf medicine!

Cannabis Indica

The vast number of Endocannabinoid receptors in our brains show our historic relationship with Cannabis may be as long as a million years. Cannabis Indica originated in continental India, and is characterized by short wide leaves, and heavy resin production.

Grown in the mountainous regions in Afghanistan and favored for the production of hashish, C. Indica is native to the northern latitude of India, and completes its cycle during the short autumns. C. Indica blooms when the long summer days shorten after the summer equinox.

C. Indica's incredible resin production during its short season has made it the choice of seers, shamans and medicine. Wise men have used it to conjure visions and provide great spiritual wisdom and powerful healing medicines for their devoted spiritual followers for thousands of years. It remains the model for Cannabis potency worldwide.

C. Indica grows well in areas north of the 40th parallel where it has adapted to wider changes in temperature, climate, and thrives easily under cooler light conditions. In the north latitudes, light duration increases in the spring, promoting vegetative growth, and in the autumn, the naturally diminishing light length and infra-red rays stimulate the plants reproductive process and force the plant into bloom and seed.

Crosses often have what is known as ***hybrid vigor,*** making them grow fast and yield well.

Under greenhouse conditions C. Indica can be easily started from seed and grown under a normal daylight regimen, and flowers in the fall.

It usually requires four to five weeks to reach sexual maturity, at which time plants may differentiate male and female. They may easily be forced into flower even before reaching mature size at six to eight weeks.

C. Indica are slightly smaller in stature, often forming a bush instead of a tree. This makes them more suitable to growing indoors. A fuller season of vegetative growth will allow them to grow to a larger size and reach their full potential.

The relative ease with which C.Indica propagates, along with its great potency and varied flavor spectrum makes it the favorite among connoisseurs. This also makes it the ideal plant for learning cultivation methods.

You may already know how to grow Cannabis

If you are looking for a familiar plant to compare to Cannabis, tomatoes would be a good fit, the nutrient requirements are much the same as Cannabis, even down to its love of magnesium. Like tomatoes, Cannabis may be easily grown outdoors in the yard or in pots on your deck or balcony, or in a small greenhouse. They don't mind a lighted closet or grow room if it is big enough and properly organized, or even being planted right in the ground, provided you put them in the right spot. A southern facing area will provide enough warmth to make very nice Cannabis bushes or a nice hedge or windbreak, and provide buds in the fall.

Fade to Black

Lemon Pledge

Chronic Concorde

Cannabis Sativa

Easy to recognize, for its elongated thin leaves and great size, Cannabis Sativa is well suited to tropical climates and is native to locations such as central America, Thailand, Africa and any of the tropical islands.

Sativa grows tall in the regular hours of the tropics, and flowers for half the year before finishing. Its herb is characterized by soaring highs and electrifying buds of gigantic proportions. Sativa can grow as tall as 20 feet, making it best suited for growing outdoors where there is a long semi- or tropical season and unlimited space.

Also occasionally known as hemp, but not to be confused with the *Cannabis Americanus* or industrial hemp, Sativa has been used for generations in its entirety, the flowers providing spiritual medicine while the fibers were used for rope, clothing, food and fuel.

In some of the tropics, C. Sativa has long been a part of the working man's ethic, where farmers in the islands do difficult and strenuous work under the heat of a tropical sun. In Jamaica, 'Ganja' breaks are known to energize and focus workers in order to physically withstand the long, hot days of exhausting labor.

How to grow Cannabis Sativa

C. Sativa is as easy to start and grow up as C. Indica, and will happily vegetate in anything over fourteen hours of light and ten dark. Unless you have twelve foot ceiling height, a greenhouse with lights, or live in the tropics, C. Sativa presents a challenge when attempting to finish it in northern latitudes. In its native latitude it often needs sixteen to twenty weeks of flowering time to complete its cycle under incredibly intense overhead sun.

Like C. Indica, it can be easily started from seed and grown under fourteen hours of light. It requires eight to twelve weeks to reach sexual maturity, and differentiate male and female. Like C. Indica, C. Sativa can be forced early.

As Sativa has the potential to be a very large plant, it is often customary to limit their height with pruning, training, or by taking cuttings and immediately flowering the small clones, thus keeping space management to a minimum. This requires the availability of cuts, a wide range of which may be available at local compassion clubs and patient advocacy organizations.

The critical point for flowering C. Sativa in nature comes when the light dips below twelve hours as fall arrives. If you are growing inside, a flowering ratio of ten hours of light and fourteen hours of darkness will trigger the plants circadian rhythm and provide the results you want.

You will notice it is slightly different from the ratio required for vegetative growth for C.Indica. A Sativa requires a great deal of patience to finish, since its long flowering time means it is at greater risk of difficulties from heat, bugs, nutrient and pH problems, and requires less nutrients. It is often recommended that C. Sativa be grown by more experienced gardeners, and I tend to agree. Discovering how Cannabis is grown is done on a sliding scale. By starting with the more straight-forward Indica strains one can learn to walk before running.

More on Hybrid Crosses: Many of the popular strains available today are the result of crossing *C. Indica* with *C. Sativa* and back crossing to stabilize the resulting progeny, based on a range of factors, such as taste, effect, size, and grow-ability. This has resulted in some great weed over the years, and the range of tastes available in a Cannabis bud is now amazing!

Cropping a Sativa for height

Zambian

UBC Chemo cross, Sativa phenotype

Females

The biological imperative of every female Cannabis plant is to catch pollen shed by the nearest males, stabilizing and reinforcing local genetics, and producing seed for the following year's progeny before it dies.

The sticky resin produced by the female has multiple purposes, protecting her from bugs and infrared radiation, and helps seal the leaves and buds to preserve water contained in the plant so it may last until the frost, and holding pollen from the males to produce seed.

When there are no male plants present, a female will continue to produce pistils and ovules long into the fall months, which if left unfertilized will become fat with protective resin glands.

The unrequited female produces Sinsimilla (American Spanish, from *sin* without + *semilla* seed) Cannabis, wand its highly potent flowers are prized for tremendous medicinal potency and a wide range of familiar flavors like coffee, chocolate, lemons, berries, and a wide range of sweet and unusual tastes from gasoline to spices.

Famous Strains & Hybrids

Afghani	Sour Diesel
Citral	Super Silver Haze
Hawaiian	Hawaiian
Skunk	Mendocino Madness
Hindu Kush	Oaxacan
Northern Lights	Malawi Gold
Swazi Skunk	Jamaican Lambsbread
Shiva	Panama Red
AK47	Super Skunk
Bubblegum	Haze
Zambian Copper	Trainwreck
Buddha	OG Kush
Jack Herer	Chem 4
Herijuana	California Orange
Panama Red	Moroccan Gold
Thai	Marley's Collie
White Rhino	New York City Diesel
Holland's Hope	Shiska Berry
Lemon Kush	Master Kush
Top 44	White Widow
Papaya	Low Ryder
Great White Shark	Colombian Gold
Big Bud	Shiva Skunk
Michoacan Gold	California Orange
Early Durban	Grapefruit
Nebula	Bubba Kush
Blueberry	Early Girl
G-13	Alaskan Thunder-Fuck
Texada Timewarp	Mango
Misty	Shiva Skunk
BC Bud	Lemon Diesel
Green Crack	Brazilian

Males

The pollen bearing male grows taller in order to pollinate as many of the surrounding females as possible. Perpetuating the species is the purpose of every growing plant, and Cannabis is no slouch in this regard.

Male flowers form in clustered bunches resembling grapes first at the leaf and branch nodes and eventually fill out and form a peak of blossoms at the terminal. Each node opens up into a white five-pointed star-shaped blossom with four dangling pods inside.

The pods quickly open and pollen is shed in the wind. Shedding continues until all the flowers have spent their pollen, and the male dies shortly after.

Seeded Cannabis flowers tend to be lower in potency than unseeded (sinsimilla) buds, because a larger portion of the plant's energy has gone into making seeds and producing progeny for the coming generation.

The males are generally removed, if possible before the flowers begin to shed their pollen, unless seed crops are desired, in which case most males will be destroyed, or select males may be allowed to pollinate to ensure passing on the best genetics for the coming generation.

If you have any designs on breeding or producing seed for the coming season, pollen may be collected from sequestered males and kept frozen for several months.

The star-shaped mature male flowers open to reveal pollen pods

Each single male flower may release thousands of pollen granules, and each one has the potential to fertilize a female and produce a seed.

Males are often discarded, since a single male can potentially fertilize thousands of female plants and unseeded crops produce superior fiber and flower. In a seed crop, the most uniform strongest males are kept to fertilize the entire field.

The grape-like clusters open into a five-pointed star formed by white petals surrounding clusters of male blossoms containing pods which will ripen and drop pollen for the wind to carry to the waiting females.

Tools and Supplies

If you are already a gardener you will probably have many of the tools, supplies and ingredients mentioned in this section already. Everyone who starts to learn growing is tempted by the vast array of specialized growing products designed to treat everything from the bugs to the roots. It is best to keep it simple and limit what you buy to basic supplies wherever possible until you actually need them. Special products can be pricey if you try to buy them all at once.

While many of these products work fine, most are simply heavily marketed, overpriced and made with simple ingredients such as molasses, various combinations of guanos, and dissolved mineral and salt-based nutrients.

Beware of grow-shop guys who are there to market products, and sell what is recommended by the manufacturer. Also, while they may appear experienced, their experience as a grower may not be relevant to your small garden since growing styles are different in a commercial situation from those in your back yard. A better candidate is a nurseryman; they generally give very good advice and supply you with the right fertilizer for your growing "tomatoes."

Pots and trays

I like the square pots for starting, for several reasons. There is less wasted space between pots, so you can put more pots into a selected growing area, use flats and trays when they are small, and they make potting up easier. Potting up diagonally to the corners provides lots of new room for the roots to grow.

Trays: For each size of pot, it's a good idea to have the right sized tray for underneath it as well. Recycled plastic lids work well. Square pots fit nicely into nursery flats, making seedlings easier to manage when they are small.

If you are on a budget, used square pots are easy to pick up at any local nursery, where they may have all sizes sorted and stacked in bins next to their greenhouse. A lot of potting up goes on during the season, and nurseries always have these on hand. Most commercial nurseries are usually glad to sell them to you for pennies each.

Nutrients + *a few other things*

- Tomato food (9-11-11)[NPK rating]
- Bloom Formula feed (6-20-10)
- Bloom Booster (0-10-10)
- Gold Standard Molasses (Mg supplement)
- Nature's Neem Oil
- Myco-Rhyzome inoculants
- Snips and scissors
- Knife or razor knife
- Moisture meter
- pH meter
- Spray bottle for misting
- A few different sizes of watering cans
- Look up NPK Rating

Most of the supplies here are easy to pick up at a nursery or gardening shop, some you may even have around the house!

THE GROWING ENVIRONMENT

THE CONSTITUENT INGREDIENTS OF GOOD SOIL

Nutrient-rich top soil

Cannabis enjoys a rich and well-draining soil. The soil you use needs to be of even consistency, organic nutrient-rich dark or black topsoil is preferred as the base. Most plant nurseries will have a custom mix on hand that they use in their propagation programs. It will have sand, soil and peat mixed in the right proportions for most seedlings. A good mix is three parts black soil, one part sand, one part peatmoss.

Perlite may be substituted for sand, which can also provide improved aeration. Your soil should be light and porous, capable of holding water and nutrients, yet easily drainable. Giving it the ability to flush the soil quickly makes it possible to correct nutrient, pH and fertilizer problems easily.

Soil conditions in a pot

In a natural setting outside and planted in the ground, nutrients and water sink past the roots and into the surrounding bacteria-rich soil regularly, which keeps the area oxygenated and precludes any toxic build-up occurring which may affect the health of the plants.

Pre-fertilized soil mixtures aren't recommended. The seedlings don't require it, and most pre-fertilized mixes are too hot for the tender seedlings, and burn them.

When a plant is growing in a pot, the situation is very different. In a container toxic buildup can occur due to the limited amount of soil supporting the ongoing aspiration of air, water and nutrients by the plant. As a result, the wastes excreted by the root system can accumulate in the pots and affect pH.

These wastes will build up to toxic levels if careful watering is not observed, eventually resulting in a rising pH, and without proper flushing can result in nutrient lock-out and leaf burn.

Watering your plants thoroughly until those acidic wastes run out the bottom of the pot is essential to maintaining a healthy pH balance in the pot.

So, even though you're using the watering through technique, checking the soil pH occasionally is still a good idea. Containerized growing has limits, due to the smaller size of the root ball, and the plant roots excrete wastes into the soil as well as breathing in and out through their leaves. The plants processes are less obvious under the soil, but conditions occurring in the pot may be read by how the top of the plant is responding.

Closely monitoring all the aspects of your plants while they are growing can only make you a better gardener by increasing your powers of observation.

Mycorrhizae Soil Bacteria

My father was an organic farmer, and told me in simple terms how it was done. I once asked how fertilizers worked, and he said to me; *"A farmer tills the soil and cares for it; tilling it to aerate, and putting back what was taken out last season. You feed the soil, and it will feed the plants. As for the plants, they know what to do. You can help by feeding the soil, but you can't make the plants grow."*

His advice didn't include the mention of nitrogen, phosphorus or other minerals; his approach was much more basic to the understanding of life. On his organic nursery, he fed the soil using natural manure, turning huge piles of composted matter rich in Mycorrhizal fungus, which he then tilled in to the land.

Soil fungi (Mycorrhizae) have a symbiotic relationship with the roots of plants. As local fungus breaks down organic matter in the soil, it also shares nutrients with the roots of plants growing in the area, feeding the micro root hairs and, by extension, the rest of the plant.

The roots sustain the Mycorrhizae by passing enzymes in return for the micro-nutrients they provide, and this relationship between fungi and plant helps both to thrive. In the absence of Mycorrhizae, plant growth can be weak and prone to other problems.

Containerized soil growing presents challenges to the balance of helpful bacteria and fungi in the soil. Since pH tends to fluctuate, soil conditions can easily become toxic and wipe out the fungal colony resulting in greatly reduced uptake of nutrients. Correct watering techniques are essential to the health of the plants, the soil and the fungi that help sustain the plant's growth processes. If soil in the pot is allowed to become toxic due to improper watering practices, the resulting problems can very quickly stunt your harvest or even ruin it. Fortunately there are easy to use Mycorrhizae formulae which may be used to re-infuse the soil with a simple watering.

The Ideal pH for Cannabis

What is the pH? This refers to the acidity or alkalinity of any growing medium or liquid relative to neutral. The middle ground or balance, known as Neutral pH, reads at 7.0 on the pH scale.

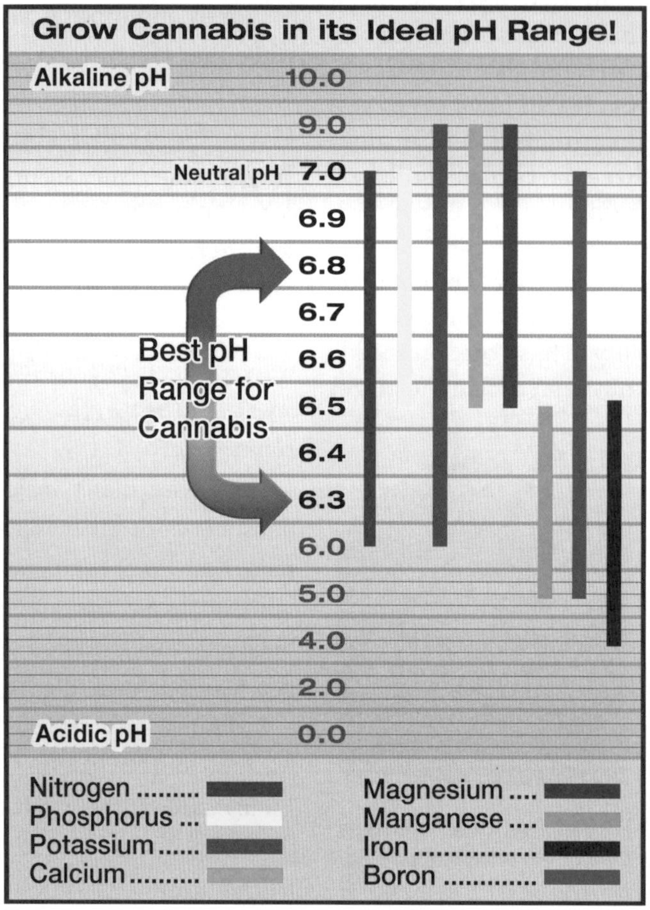

The correct pH in any growing medium is essential to maintaining the steady uptake of nutrients to support healthy and vigorous plant growth.

Cannabis enjoys a slightly *acidic pH*, best suited to grow in the range between pH 6.6 and pH 6.9 where Nitrogen **(N)** Phosphorus **(P)** Potassium, **(K)** Magnesium, **(Mg)** and Calcium **(Ca)** can be efficiently absorbed through the roots.

At pH levels of 6.5 and lower, excessive acidity will prevent plants from being able to absorb all five of the main essential nutrients, 'locking' the plants nutrient uptake so it can't feed on what may still be available in the soil.

Checking the pH levels at the source of your water with a hand meter is an excellent practice, so if the pH range is too high (8.0 and up) or too low (6.5 or less) you may need to adjust it or select a more neutral water source for your gardening. I like rain water.

The pH in a container plant can drop into acidity as the plant throws off waste from the roots, but good common daily gardening practice can help prevent this. Watering all your plants through a bit, so those acidic wastes run out the bottom of the pot, is extremely helpful to maintaining a healthy pH in the pot and keeping your plants growing happily. That being said, even if you manage pH with good watering, checking your soil pH occasionally is still a good idea. Close monitoring of all the aspects of your plant environment can only make you a better gardener.

Excessive Alkalinity: In most cases severe alkalinity is caused by the build-up of minerals and/or salinity in the medium, from the use of salt-sourced fertilizers or a mineralized water source such as an artesian well. The presence of saline soil conditions prevents root-friendly Myco-Rhyzome bacteria in the soil from thriving. Once the symbiotic soil bacteria is killed, the plants nutrient uptake is greatly diminished. In extreme cases highly mineralized mediums can cause hooked leaves and severe leaf tip burn and spots on the main leaves. Organic fertilizers made from seaweed, guano and other naturally sourced nutrients tend to be less problematic, as they are fed in lower doses and used by the plant sooner, so they are less prone to building up in the soil.

Solution: Potentially the affected plants may require repotting with new soil. Flush with neutrally balanced water until PPM is as low as possible and then use an infusion to replace the Myco-Rhyzome along with an organic fertilizer to feed. (Good old *guano*)

Excessive Acidity: Usually the cause of an excessively acid soil environment is not so much the build up of additives, but simply the use of containers and the natural excretions through the roots of the plants, and is the natural result of plant processes. The plant wastes leaving the roots, which in nature would be flushed away with every rain build up and accumulate in the restricted pot. Good watering technique can help minimize the problem, allowing the pot to leak properly with each watering. Flushing will show a yellow discoloration to the runoff.

Solution: Flush with neutrally balanced water until the brown to yellow runoff runs clear, and the PPM is low as possible, and then replace the Myco-Rhyzome along with an organic fertilizer to feed. Apply Molasses Drench comprised of one teaspoon molasses to a gallon of water for magnesium, and fertilize half strength and observe.

LIGHTING SPECTRUM

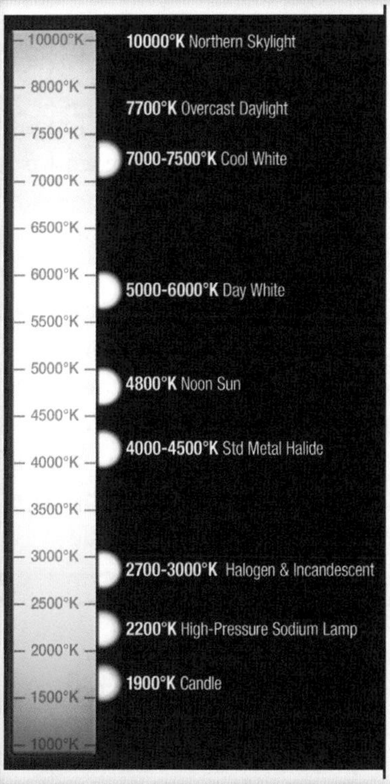

Lighting Temperatures/Color, Types and Uses

°K/Color	Type of Lighting	Best Use
5900K	T5 Fluorescents	Seedlings/Clones
5500K/Blue	Daylight Metal Halide	Vegetative
4000-4200K white to blue	Cool white Fluorescent	Seedlings/Clones
3800-4800K/yellow to White	Compact Fluorescent	Seedlings/Clones
4000K	Std Clear Metal Halide	All purpose
3200K	Warm Metal Halide	All purpose
3000K/Yellow	Halogen Lamps	Not suited to growing
2500K	Standard Incandescent	Not suited to growing
2200K/Orange	High Pressure Sodium	Vegetative/Flowering
2100K	HPS/MH conversion bulbs	Vegetative/Flowering

Good lights/Bad lights: Some lights may be well suited for brightening a room, but not for growing, such as in the case of standard incandescent and Halogen lights, which use the wrong spectrum for growing. Also not mentioned above is the Mercury Halide is not very well suited to Cannabis growing. Cannabis will grow best under full spectrum lighting of extremely high intensity from maturity to the end of its flowering season.

During the natural course of a growing season, the light will go through changes, both in duration and spectrum. In the north, the increasing spring light will phase from red to blue as it lengthens into summer, while the waning fall light will shift from blue back through red as the days become shorter.

If you are growing outside in the yard, deck or other naturally lighted area, you may have the option of allowing the season to handle the lighting frequency, while you manage water, nutrients and potting up for the plants all through the growing season. However, if you are growing in an inside space, you will need to understand how this works so you may properly recreate the ideal conditions.

Lighting for seedlings

Early lighting for new seedlings can easily and safely be done under compact, T5 or regular fluorescent lights, as their lighting frequency most closely resembles the early spring light. Compact Fluorescent lights use a great deal less energy, don't make a lot of heat, and are a very efficient light for seedlings and small plants. Using High Intensity Discharge lighting on seedlings can be risky before four weeks of age, since although they are very efficient and bright lights, they create a lot of heat as well, more than enough to cook a tender seedling.

From Adolescent to Mature plants

Once the plant is past the two to three week mark and doing well, taking up nutrients and putting on foliage, the volume of light must increase to reflect the growing season (simulating the higher summer sun) and to accommodate the ever increasing foliage. The plant will be increasing in size at a tremendous rate, and this is the critical time when it needs energy to reach maturity. Combination Metal Halide and HPS lights can add the additional light needed to simulate a summer day, as well as providing a dramatic increase in lumen volume, giving the plant the energy needed to reach fully mature stature.

Bringing on the Autumn

The natural course in nature is a gradual drop in light length, accompanied by the slow shift from blue into the red spectrum as fall signals the Cannabis plant to begin blooming. Under lights, you have considerably more control over the lighting and environment, so you can mix daylight halides with high pressure sodium light for full spectrum light.

Successful growing depends on rising light volume and shifting color frequency from blues to reds to properly simulate nature. High Pressure Sodium lights tend to outperform the Metal Halide lamp, typically adding 20% to the lumen output when replacing equivalent wattage. This makes them the ideal lighting for vegetating in combination with metal halide, or flowering Cannabis, since they also effectively provide the additional light volume required for maximizing the yield of your plants.

Photo-Periodic Control Lighting

During the course of growing Cannabis, I have noticed negative effects such as poor plant health and clone burn-out while using eighteen-hour lighting. Once I began using the 12-1 vegetation, I noticed a marked increase in the health and vitality of all my Cannabis plants. This suggested to me that over-lighting during vegetation stresses the plants, making the health and genetics of the clones and seedlings degrade over the course of several generations.

The Natural Cycles: Eighteen straight hours of full natural lighting is nowhere to be found (unless you count the Polar latitudes, but I don't see much weed growing there). In northern areas where the summer is short, outdoor lighting is no longer than fifteen to sixteen hours total, fine for outdoor growing. During a recent discussion with Joe Pietri, he introduced me to an old technique. (Paul V. Nelson: Greenhouse Management) It is a method known as the 12-1 lighting, which nurtures the plant to its fullest potential, and increases yield and genetic strength while using decreased light hours.

The 'cash cropping' method of cultivation I first learned employs a schedule of eighteen hours on and six off during the Vegetative stage, and flowering is triggered using twelve on and twelve off. My under-performing plants made it apparent to me this lighting schedule is counterproductive, and trying the 12-1 showed it was unnecessary to over-light to produce fully healthy and productive plants. 18-6 lighting just does not recognize the plant's need for an adequate dark period, and over-exposure to light is harmful.

Crops under these 'hard labor' schedules typically under-perform in taste, yield, health and potency. Study nature a little and you can see that from the point of view of the stationary plant, the sun gradually moves from east to west, casting light and shadows on the plant from objects in front, beside, and behind it during the course of the day. Out in the natural environment the play of light and shadow across the leaves are important to the natural processes of the plant. This information may seem counter-intuitive to growers who now produce Cannabis, seemingly with little or no trouble at all. In fact, plants may be maintained in vegetative cycle using only a total of thirteen hours of light daily, reducing production cost 30%.

Reduced lighting in the flower stage provides even more savings, and it is well known that plants naturally grow during dark periods as well. Standard flowering calls for twelve hours of lighting, but ten hours will produce a stronger response due to the buildup of light sensitive hormones.

Seedlings and Cuttings: This is where the longest schedule is used, and the only appropriate place for a schedule of sixteen hours of light, and eight hours of dark. Lighting for seedlings needs to be bright and close, (200w-400w CFL rating) while much less lighting is needed for rooting cuttings in order to promote roots rather than growth. (40w is adequate for rooting).

The Vegetative Schedule: As illustrated by the graph, this method is quite simple: 12 hours of light, followed by five and one half hours of darkness, a single hour of light, and a second period of five-and-one-half hours of darkness to complete the twenty-four-hour cycle.

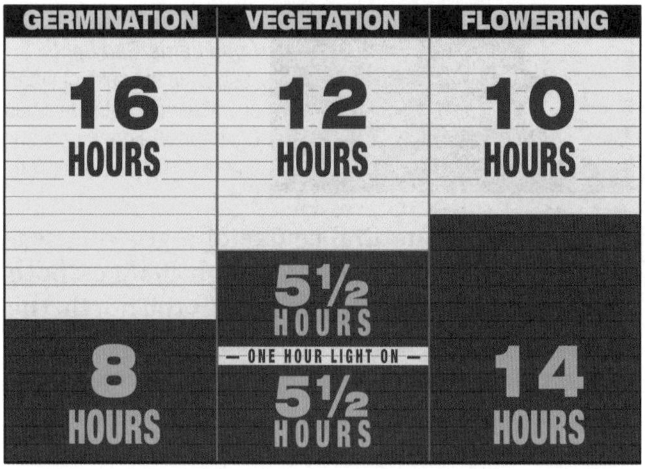

The full hour of light in the middle of a twelve hour dark period interrupts the buildup up of floral hormones which prevents them from triggering flowers and keeps the plants growing in the vegetative state. The grower simply raises his rooted plants to the desired size, before switching to the fall schedule to bloom.

Using this method, the length of the vegetative cycle may even be reduced, and with a shorter growth cycle comes a tremendous reduction in power consumption, more frequent crop rotation and better production. It is even possible to add another grow cycle to your year with the additional weeks.

12-1 Issues: During spring or cool weather conditions, vegetating plants can sometimes still flower under 12-1, so to prevent this the one hour interruption of light may need to be lengthened by a half hour or more to ensure that phytochromes are properly suppressed.

Photo-periodic light control is a proven technique used by commercial flower growers to earn billions growing chrysanthemums, poinsettias and other flowers we enjoy in our homes and gardens every day!

12-12 Schedule

12-12 Drawbacks

- Date is July 21st, in the summer. It's not time to flower.
- 12-12 is responsible for additional internode stretching and only partially flowers the plant.
- 12-12 Wastes energy: causes plants to over-use nutrients that would otherwise go further in the flowering season, requiring more be used to finish.
- 12-12 lighting is not short enough to fully engage flowering, leaving it partially in a vegetative state.
- Additional leaf grown requires extra trimming labor, increasing production cost.

18-6 Schedule

18-6 Drawbacks

- Overly long light skews growth and wastes fertilizer and energy.
- 6 hours is too short a rest period, secondary branches don't develop.
- Flowering hormones are over suppressed and light stress causes severe stem and in-ternode stretching.
- Excess heat produced also causes stress, and requires additional cooling and venting to correct. This is expensive!
- 18-6 is only useful for regenerative growth on previously flowered plants.
- 18 hours of light is unnatural, and harms the plants with over exposure to radiation (light), causing stress reactions such as in-ternode stretching, and required that plants be over-fertilized in order to survive.

18-6 Requires Two Suns!

A little thought eventually revealed that an eighteen hour day would require that more than half of a spherical globe such as our earth would have to be lit at once. This top-down simulation clearly shows how it would take two light sources to provide 18 hours of light on any spherical globe. A single point of light (such as our sun) can only light so much of the earth at one time, as seen in the second figure, exactly half, or twelve hours.

18-6 increases the cost of growing by wasting energy and requiring unusual measures to sustain, such as overfertilization and heat exhaustion.

Eighteen hours of light is unnatural, and harms the plants with over exposure to radiation (light), causing stress reactions such as internode stretching, and required that plants be overfertilized in order to survive.

PFR Phytochromes and How They Work

PFR Phytochromes are a light sensitive chemical responsible for controlling a plant's season and reproduction. Flowering begins when Phytochromes build up beyond a saturation threshold. Cannabis flowers when PFR threshold has been reached.

By suppressing or allowing PFR phytochromes to build up, flowering or vegetation can be controlled. Over suppression of PFR's is stressful to your plants and concentrates growth to the terminals.

Allowing longer nights or using 12-1 lets PFR's fluctuate in normal levels, distributing more useful energy to the center of the plant, and increasing overall plant output.

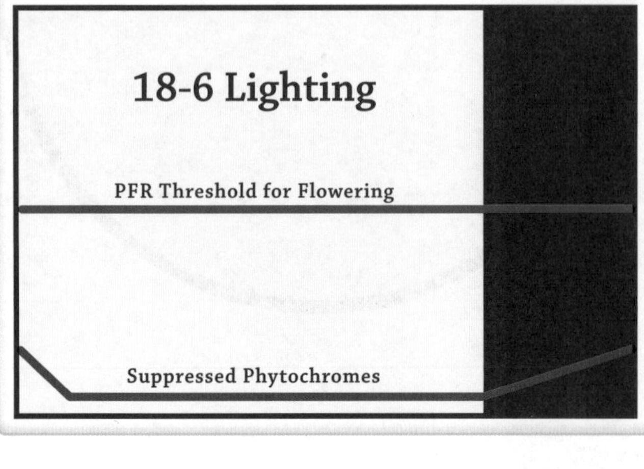

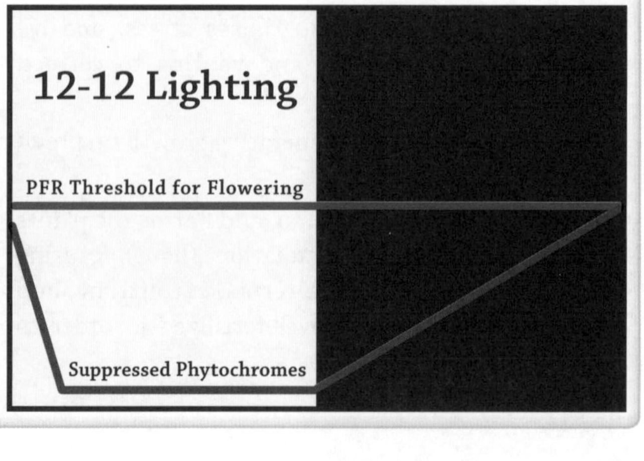

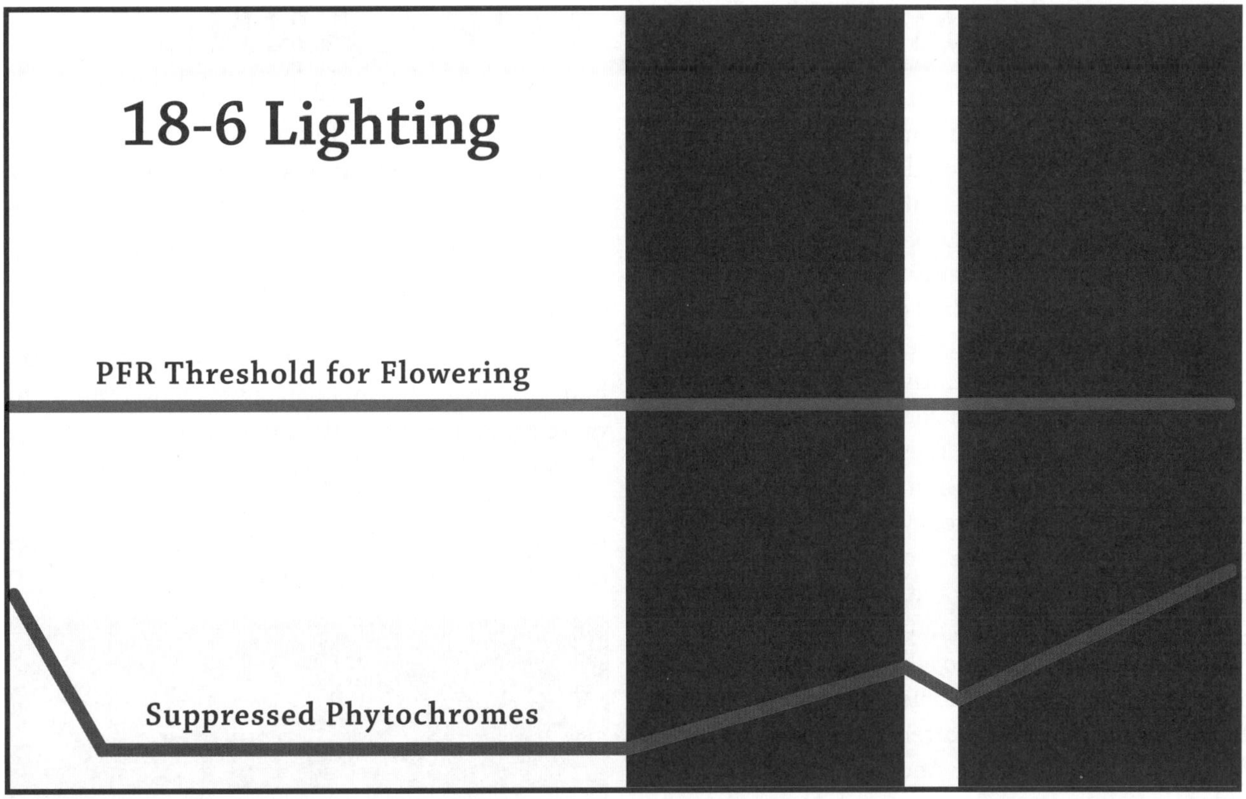

The 12-1 schedule allows PFR to rise and fall during Veg, but keeps plants well below the flowering threshold.

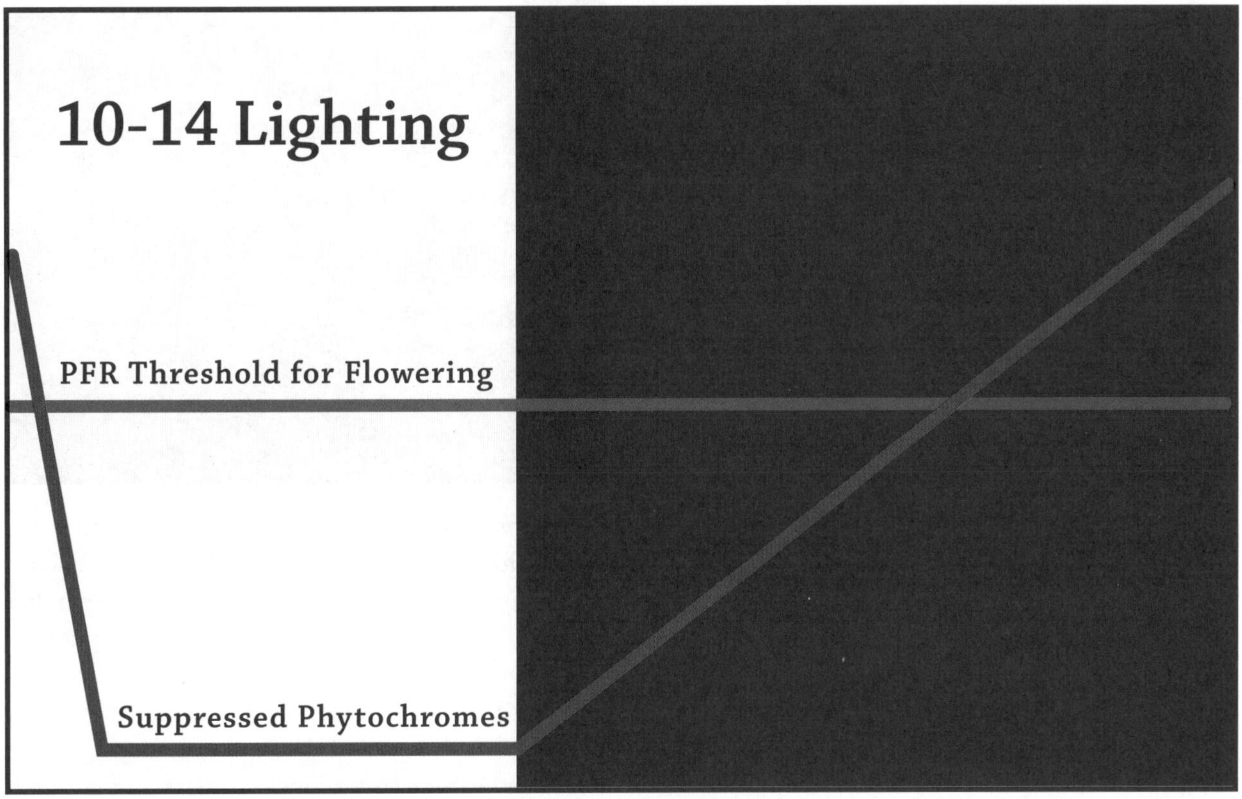

10-14 pushes PFR levels far beyond the PFR threshold stopping stem and leaf production and concentrating energies on flowering.

12-1 AND 10-14 FOR CANNABIS

Some thoughts from Boo

First of all, thanks for taking the time out of your life to read this personal account. I believe the information contained in this book is important - the Cannabis plant has been revered by mankind throughout our long and fairly arduous history. It has provided for us over countless generations, only in recent decades has it come under attack as a perceived threat to society. The real motives behind this massive stone walling are questionable, look into it yourself for a clearer view. I believe these archaic laws to be at the detriment of all who live in the legacy of a "war on drugs" that still rages on today. Given what we know now, or have always known about the medicinal qualities of Cannabis, how can a state funded war on the sick and ill at ease ever be helpful, or lawful?

In the science fiction novel Pallas, one of L. Neil Smith's characters says, "People—pardon me, journalists and politicians—have often accused me of believing that I'm above the law. And yet, who isn't? ... The law is created by demonstrable criminals, enforced by demonstrable criminals, interpreted by demonstrable criminals, all for demonstrably criminal purposes. Of course I'm above the law. And so are you." Essentially, if you must take matters into your own hands by necessity, nothing should stand in the way. An outlaw is not automatically a criminal, however the law will not protect you. This can present problems for an otherwise law abiding medical cannabis user, especially in the case of personal cultivation "for the purpose of trafficking" (a crime of presumed guilt which in itself is unlawful).

Since I was eighteen, I have lived with Fibromyalgia. It's a commonly misunderstood condition. Related to chronic fatigue syndrome, it is usually preceded by a serious viral infection. In my lucky case this was Epstein Barr virus (glandular fever), though the virus was eventually overcome the constant nagging pains continued. I was recreational weekend user (the drinking culture seemed daft) and I found that an (apparent) side effect was improved wellbeing and reduced inflammation. So, it turns out it's really the only thing that can bring back the quality of life taken for granted before becoming ill. While the condition is not life threatening, it feels like a life sentence for those who are experience it. Getting a diagnosis is one thing, treating it is another matter entirely.

I used lots of other drugs, such as stimulants, pain killers and Alcohol. This landed me up in terrible emotional pain and also partially "cooked" in the head. My wife left with my two children never to return. Thankfully I have a good relationship with my boys, but it is very regrettable. I can hardly blame her considering what a fucking train-wreck I had become. I can only keep moving forward, hopefully remaining partially unaffected. Hope is a tragic thing to lose. All I use for fibro now is Cannabis, and I was pleased to hear my buddy Morgan Freeman in agreement (and a much more convincing voice than my own - playing God and all) about Fibromyalgia pain. There is also mounting evidence on the nerve regeneration and protective capabilities of other cannabinoids, which could theoretically play a role in recovery for addicts.

Being scorned for your choice of medication is a kind of emotional abuse, particularly when there is no alternative for you but to get on with life and take pills and ethanol. Try codeine constipation, or dexamphetamine come down. Some of us end up addicts, so I trade "dependence" happily and with gratitude. In the end, Cannabis is what works and that is the bottom line for me. I took my garden behind locked doors and got started years ago now. If you are producing medicine only for yourself, provided you are not terminally ill, very little equipment is needed to start a medical garden.

What you have learned in this book is the best growing practice. Commercial market gardeners employ these trade secrets, season after season to the tight deadlines required of the wholesale plant industry. There is no unique botany for Cannabis, it shares its traits with the rest of its species and derives its many variations by climatic zone. It is a short day, long night plant. Of course, it remains illegal in most parts of the world.

Many seasoned gardeners might hesitate making the switch at first, but be assured that when you make your move to 12-1, your garden will change only in positive ways. From the outset you will save five hours off the common 18/6. Twenty-four hour lighting is complete overkill, but if you've adopted this practice your savings are even more dramatic. Reducing lighting hours means less heat and less stress, which in turn can mean less water and feeding. If you are just starting out - this is the best start you can have. You won't get bogged down in nonsense and you'll know the difference between bullshit and proven science.

The switch to 10-14 should always be preceded by 12-1, the hormone levels peaked by photoperiodic control result in fast onset flowering and trichomes production, without the use of PGR (plant growth regulators). While reducing flowering time by 2 hours doesn't represent as much of a significant saving, it pays off in both yield and quality. You may even be able to harvest your crop earlier and you can now finish Sativas properly indoors - this is a fundamental step forward as you can now grow practically any strain indoors in a reasonably short timeframe.

I have experimented with reducing hours further, to a minimum of 6. In my own experience with Indica dominant strains, six was too little, producing less yield overall. Ten seems optimal, but I believe further reduction is possible. Below eight hours could produce low yields, particularly with Indicas. As you work more with this technique and your preferred strains, the balance between stress and enjoyment starts to tip heavily in your favour. A renewed sense of control over your garden and some of the best nugs you'll ever taste - you won't be turning back to the old ways. In fact, your time growing before now will be forgotten. I sometimes see pictures of the old 12/12 garden, plants I thought at the time to be of decent quality were really quite stressed, stretched and thirsty. Stretching is caused by the dramatic light reduction from eighteen or twenty four to twelve. It does not occur in the same way using a 12-1 schedule, allowing you to veg longer without zombie headroom paranoia.

Growth patterns are different, the plant is literally one hour away from bloom and they take on nice compact shapes. It is unnecessary and detrimental to prune or FIM plants, it leaded to excessive branching and a pain in the arse trimming. Expect tighter nodes, wider, bushier plants with excellent structure. Previously FIM was almost a necessity with the exception of SCROG growing perhaps. Now, the natural shapes of the plant are ideal for indoor growing.

While it is often recommended to use 16-8 (as an absolute maximum in any situation) to raise seeds and clones, it's not completely necessary. Cloning with 100% success from 12-1 mothers is relatively simple. Existing mothers can be re-conditioned to this schedule by stepping to 16-8 for a few weeks. The myth about hermaphroditism triggered by photoperiod is rubbish - your genetics determine this trait. Unfortunately, the market is flooded with questionable seed stock. Find a good breeder - don't use crappy Dutch sites. While stress can cause this trait, it should not be commonly showing under any fixed light regime.

I hope that this technique will bring even more positive feedback from your plants. As you observe the results, I'm sure you will love what you see unfolding. Combining this knowledge with good plant nursing will see your crop reach its full potentials unhindered. Your plants will thrive, stress free. Potentially you can too if you want to, there really isn't much to it. Just a willingness to take a new approach to something you may have thought you already knew is enough. Regardless of your preferred medium, fertiliser or lighting sources, this science based method will give you happier, more potent plants.

Happy Gardening!

Boo

12-1 Growing

When I was asked to write my thoughts about the 12-1, I was delighted, for two reasons! First, I'm thrilled to be part of such an awesome group, and secondly I used to be such a skeptic especially in regards to my gardening techniques.

I have been a gardener for most of my life, actually over half. When I first started growing and learned the basics on how things were grown, I became hooked! I first began learning and researching as much as I possibly could on how to make my plants grow to their full potential.

I'm a very much a hands on Gardner, I feel the techniques and formulas I have read and learn need to be put to the test. I've had many successes and many failures so, I took all this great research and decided this was how I was going to grow, and I was happy I had finally found the perfect combination.

When I first heard of the 12-1 method, I realized I needed to find out more about this and be more open-minded! The 12-1 has shown me, you're never too old to stop learning. As I went on I didn't want to miss out on anything that could possibly enhance my growing abilities. The 12-1 was very different than I was used to, but I needed to take a step back and reevaluate.

The 12-1 works for the vegetative cycles. The cycle is very basic 12 hours on, 5 1/2 hours off, one hour on, at 5 1/2 hours off again. This is for the veg cycle! The bloom cycle or flower cycle is a little more detailed.

The first two weeks you have 11 hours on and 13 hours off! Weeks three and four 10 1/2 hours on and 13 1/2 hours off Weeks five and six 10 1/2 hours on 14 off. Weeks seven through eight 9 1/2 hours on 13 1/2 hours off and nine hours on and 15 hours off until you have completed your harvests.

It's somewhat involved but after you've done it and get the hang of it becomes easy. It's actually genius not only can you save on your energy cost, but you can increase your yield as well. It's actually a win-win situation. It's my hope that everyone who hears of this method will utilize it and grasp it with open arms.

It's not just a theory but a proven to be true fact. To become a very competent gardener and a true lover of growing you need to pursue all avenues of knowledge. As a gardener you can always determine for yourself what actually the best is for you.

Its rather disheartening that the industry has put such a high price on the different mediums and growing tools etc. for you, because there are a lot of crazy concept and gimmicks out there, some are worthy, and some just are that gimmicks.

That's why it's rather refreshing to learn about 12/1. It shouldn't cost us an arm and a leg today to increase our plants potential growing.

Howard W.

Six Schedules for Growing

Overlighting the plants has its place; note that in schedule six it is used for regenerating fully flowered plants. Slightly overlighting the plants early in growth can make for a faster start for seedlings, so I recommend multiple schedules to accomplish the full cycle from beginning to end: Sixteen hours of lighting, and tight, bright spaces prior to entering the 12-1 vegetation period, then a triggering period of 10-14 followed by finishing the flowering cycle at 9-15 to induce extreme buildup in the flowering hormones (PFR Phytochromes).

The six lighting schedules I use and the benefits of using each of them:

1. Seedlings (Four-week period)
16 hours on, 8 hours off

- An extended warm period draws the seedling out and gives them a quick start.
- Shortens the adolescent period as much as 2 weeks.

2. Vegetation (optional length period, as short as 4 weeks, or up to 6 months) — **12 hours on, 5 ½ off, 1 hour on, 5 ½ off,** cycled over a 24 hour period.

- High lighting stress on the plant is greatly reduced.
- Interruption of one-hour of light prevents the plant from building up enough phytochromes to go into flower.
- The production of inside foliage is dramatically increased, making cuttings much more numerous.
- Plants are much easier to trigger, and immediately flower when lighting is changed.

3. Cuttings (Two-week period, Rockwool cubes, #2 rooting powder)
16 hours on, 8 hours off

- Light dropped to 40w CFL to slow photosynthesis.
- Humidity dome environment keeps everything moist while roots form.

4. Flowering (Half the normal flowering period for the strain)
10 hours on, 14 hours off

- Flowers are triggered immediately within a day or two.
- Internodal stretching is prevented.
- Flower production is increased.
- Leaf production is inhibited.

5. Finishing (Half the normal flowering period for the strain minus 20%)
9 hours on 15 hours off

- PFR phytochromes are allowed to build up to intense levels in the plant.
- Leaf production stops entirely.
- Pistil production increases, making buds grow sideways.
- Oils are exposed to less light and therefore remain more potent.
- Plant will usually finish up prior to normal finish time.

6. Regeneration (Its after flowering and you want clones)
18 hours on, 6 hours off

- Destroys PFR Phytochromes and allows the plant to re-enter vegetation stage.
- A shot of Nitrogen reboots the cell building process.

Comparing 18-6 and 12-1 Power Use

18-6 Growing

Seedlings (18-6) 4 weeks
4 x 200w (42w) cfl's (168w)
.168 x 18 = 3.024 kWh day
3.024 x 30 = **90.72** kWh month

Vegetation (18-6) 4 weeks
(10 x 200w cfl's) (42w)
.420 x 18 = 7.56 kWh day
7.56 x 30 = **226.8** kWh month

Flowering (12-12) 8 weeks
1 x 400w High Pressure Sodium
.4 x 12 = 4.8 kWh day
4.8 x 60 (2 mo.) = **288** kWh (144 kWh mo.)

Total kWh: 605.52

12-1 Photoperiodic Growing

Seedlings (16-8) 4 weeks
4 x 200w (42w) cfl's (168w)
.168 x 16 = 2.688 kWh day
2.688 x 30 = **80.64** kWh mo.

Vegetation (12-1) 4 weeks
10 x 200w cfl's (42w)
.420 x 13 = 5.46 kWh day
5.46 x 30 = **163.8** kWh mo.

Flowering (10-14), 4 weeks
1 x 400w High Pressure Sodium
.4 x 10 = 4 kWh day
4 x 30 = **120** kWh mo.

Finishing (9-15), 4 weeks
1 x 400w High Pressure Sodium
.4 x 9 = 3.6 kWh day
3.6 x 30 = **108** kWh mo.

Total kWh: 472.44

133.08 kWh saved or **22% less** power used!

AIR & WATER

As every plant does, Cannabis breathes in oxygen through its leaves, and expels C02 through its roots. Its long and fibrous taproots break up the soil it is growing in, and C02 is allowed to enter the soil through the cracks and get rinsed away with precipitation.

The entire root system is about the same size as the top of the plant, and extends as far as the tips of the plants leaves.

In the natural setting of your back yard, thermal currents and updrafts provide wind that is blown over the many leaves and passes though stomata where it is taken in. In the same manner as Cannabis breathes through its leaves, CO2 exhausted through the roots.

Indoors, you must make sure there is enough wind blowing the air around your growing area to reasonably approximate wind that occurs in a natural biosphere. Forced air from oscillating fans will provide air movement inside the space, and stale air also needs to be replaced with fresh air drawn in from outside. Heat produced by the lamps is normally drawn out at the top of the space, while passive intake near the floor draws in cool and fresh air from outside.

What happens when it rains?

In the outside environment, the thermal currents in the atmosphere create water vapors, and it condenses and begins falling as rain. The raindrops hit the ground and soaks the soil. As the water sinks down through the soil, the CO2 released by the plant's roots is pushed out by the moisture. If you have ever noticed the smell of the earth after a good rain, it is from CO2 being expelled from the soil. A well-watered pot will release the same smell as the water soaks the soil and drives out the old gases, and draws in moisture to the roots of your plants. A fresh spurt of growth always follows a summer rain, or a good watering.

Without any water, there can be no growth – it could not be any simpler than that. Water is the great provider, bringing oxygen and nutrients, sustaining moisture, removing waste build-up and hydrating the plant, and making growth possible. Neither too much nor too little will do.

In nature wastes sink past the roots when it rains. When you are growing in pots, you have to flush your plants every few weeks to avoid toxic buildup.

A good watering technique will simultaneously rinse away plant wastes left behind by the roots, pull fresh air into the soil and help maintain a healthy pH balance.

Water well, so as to completely hydrate the root-ball, and allow a small amount of water to run out the bottom to partially flush out plant wastes. Lifting the pot to test its weight is a very effective method of seeing how fast each plant uses water. Not all of your plants will use water at the same rate.

Room Humidity

The preferred humidity for your plants may vary slightly on the strain, but the ideal range of humidity for the happiness of Cannabis is typically between fifty and sixty percent in the daytime, and 75-80 percent in the night-time hours.

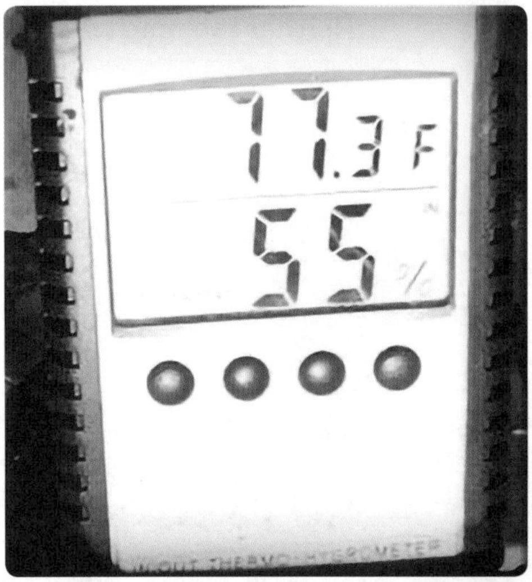

A room humidistat such as the one pictured to the right is essential equipment for monitoring the humidity content of your growing spaces. Naturally the grow-room must be an encapsulated area, sealed to moisture so the environment can be closely monitored and manipulated at will.

Managing your grow-room humidity must be done manually in the early part of the grow cycle when the plants are small, since they don't yet have the ability to regulate and take control of their environment. Intake for fresh air and fan circulation can be managed using a thermostat circuit to exhaust or recycle excess heat, dehumidify and draw in cooler fresh air.

During early vegetation, spraying the walls and floor when humidity drops below fifty percent is essential to keep the plants growing in an ideal and comfortable environment, so there will be no interruption in their growth patterns.

Once the plants have reached full size and height, their increased leaf area will give them the ability to easily self-correct room humidity. Observe how during the day cycle, opening the door to enter a room can drop the humidity. You can see it drop briefly using the humidistat, and then after a few minutes, how it rises again. As the plants react to the drop in humidity, they increase transpiration and healthy, growing plants will work to re-establish the desired ideal humidity.

An environment that is too dry also invites some unwanted guests, as well. In particular, Spider-mites like a dry environment to live in, and keeping the environment comfortable for plants but uncomfortable for bugs is the goal in room management. You will see how your plants respond positively, The indication that your plants are "happy" will be the upright top leaves, and rapid growth.

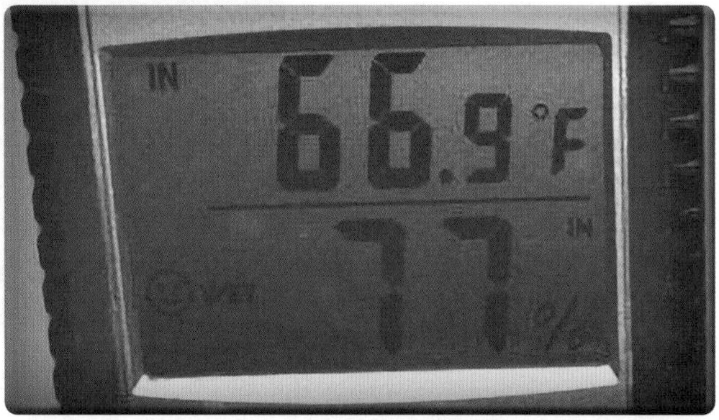

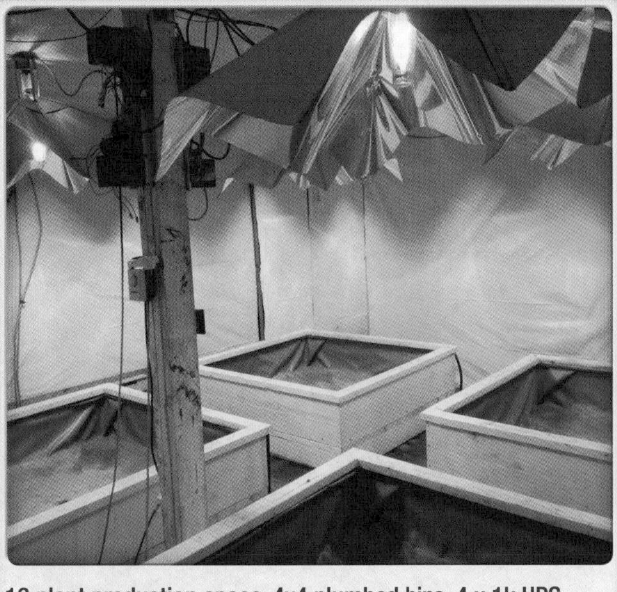

16 plant production space, 4x4 plumbed bins, 4 x 1k HPS

Happy plants characterized by rapid growth & deep color.

Nutrients for Cannabis

Nitrogen (N) is the first number in the NPK rating scale; you will see it printed on all fertilizer. It is the most common nutrient all plants need to grow, as it provides some of the main building blocks for cell production and photosynthesis, the production of chlorophyll, and converting energy for the seasons growth. Nitrogen is used to a greater degree during the vegetative stage, but is an essential element at all stages of growth.

Phosphorous (P) is the nutrient that Cannabis uses the most of during the entire reproductive season. A typical blooming formula has a high middle number, and the first and third are low. For example, 6/20/10 is a common organic guano-based flower bed blooming formula which works just fine for M.J.

Potassium (K) is one of the important building blocks for all growth, especially in the formative stages of the plant's life. In the fall, when the source of potassium naturally drops due to rain leaching the surrounding soil, this helps to trigger the flowering mechanism. This is why you'll see that most bloom formulas have a lower last number, due to the decreased levels of Potassium.

CAUTION: Fertilizing too often can cause a dangerous salt build-up in the soil container, which can potentially affect the pH of the soil, and prevent the uptake of other nutrients as well as causing severe burning to the leaves.

Magnesium Deficiency causes leaf edge curling in the early phases. Left uncorrected, plants will become brittle and suddenly drop all their leaves and die very quickly.

When and how to fertilize

Fertilizers are used to replace nutrients and minerals that exist in the soil and become depleted as the plants grow. Plants will use nutrients in different measures throughout the growing season, using water and nutrients faster as they become larger and develop more complex root systems.

Seedlings: in fresh soil mix should not need any fertilizer, but as they grow, they will deplete these nutrients, and around three weeks into growth they may turn pale green or yellow, and require nutrients in the soil be replenished.

Adolescent and Mature plants: A high nitrogen organic growth formula is needed, and for most of the grow a *fish-based tomato formula* drench may be used without any trouble every couple of weeks until the plant reaches maturity and/or the desired size.

Flowering plants: the natural needs of Cannabis start with a dropping Nitrogen level. Once the plant has reached sexual maturity it can be given elevated Phosphorus and potassium to promote flower and bud growth.

Organic nutrients: being lower in concentration and made from natural sources like guanos, they are easy to under-use. Use generously, and follow directions for full strength outdoor growing plants. Reapply when you observe yellowing in the leaves.

Molasses Recipe: One-time application, dissolve one tablespoon of Gold Standard unsulfured pure molasses in one cup of hot water, and add to 2 gallons of water. Soak the soil when dry for full uptake. Molasses contains natural sugars, Mg, and Ca, all of which support plant requirements and feeds the soil Mycorrhiza.

Dolomite Lime: 1/4 cup of dolomite lime added to every ten gallons of soil mix prior to planting will normally supply Magnesium for the entire growing season.

SEEDS

Carefully select your seed

When you buy seed, you should do some research into the properties of the strain you want, to ensure it will do what you wish it to do. This is especially important for patients hoping to use Cannabis as medicine. All Cannabis has varying levels of THC, CBD, CBN, and other important medical compounds, some of which are more useful for treating specific symptoms. You would not puff an energetic Sativa if you need to sleep – a sedative Indica would be more effective. It is responsible usage to understand the effects of the Cannabis you're growing, so it will help you manage your symtoms effectively.

Cannabis seeds are now widely available online in an astonishing array of flavors and strains and price ranges from reputable seed shops in Canada, Holland, the UK and many other countries where they allow Cannabis seeds to be sold. Even though countries like the US try to prevent seed from entering the country, companies still manage to deliver worldwide using stealthy mailing techniques to ensure safe delivery.

If you are planning to use the Cannabis you grow for medicine, ask the vendor to give you information on the genetics; a decent seed seller knows the genetics of his strains. Beware, there are some unscrupulous dealers out there who will sell any old seed and call it some fancy name. The same goes for dispensaries, many Cannabis patients have been disappointed when the product they grew was not as advertized. It is really just safer to get seeds from a reputable source who knows the seed's lineage and can offer strains best suited to your needs.

You also can get your beans from some good Cannabis, but you will need to inspect them for viability. Bear in mind that in the present era of cloned and mass-produced sinsimilla, any seeds you find can potentially be the product of stressed plants in someone's commercial grow room.

A viable seed should be dark, round, shiny, and uniform in shape, with a slight indentation at one end, and pointed at the other. They range in color from green to black, may be striped or without, have spots, be tiny in size or even big and fat looking.

If you find some herb that you like with seeds in it, go ahead and use them. You already have an idea what the end product is like, so that makes a great place to start.

If you start 10 or so, you should get enough females to get a nice starter crop. (If you saved all the seeds

from one kind of bud in its own container, congratulations! You can have some fun breeding.

Cannabis seeds

The Cannabis seed is a very uniquely structured grain seed, with two round half shells hermetically sealed together at the edges to house the tender inner genetic package. As seeds get older, this shell may toughen, making the seeds stubborn to sprout, however they will remain viable as long as the shell remains sealed. Cracks or deformities in the shell will desiccate it, and kill the sprout inside.

Techniques for germination may include a process known as *scarification.* One method uses sandpaper in a match box, or a wet tumbler may be used to thin the shell and allow moisture to penetrate the seed shell and activate growth before dropping them in a glass of water to hydrate. Germination has occurred when the root begins to poke out of the pointed end of the seed shell.

Landraces and hybrids

These are terms you will commonly hear in regard to where seeds have originated. A landrace is a strain that has lived in a remote area, sometimes for hundreds of years and become inbred to the point of complete uniformity. In most cases a breeder will begin with landraces for the production of hybrid strains. The purity and strong genes of a landrace strain make it highly prized, both for its original medical qualities, and for its clean breeding opportunities.

A hybrid strain can often show quite a lot of variability in plant size and characteristics depending on its lineage. Such is the nature of mixed genetics, with back crossing they can achieve some uniformity, but like a landrace, many generations of back crossing are required for the plant to become uniform. A positive attribute of hybrids is that clean crosses often possess what is known as 'hybrid vigor' which gives them amazing growth. The genetic mix of a hybrid can produce many desirable flavors and incredible potency, which are then often reproduced as clones.

Deciphering Seeds and Strain Crosses

P1 Landrace

P1 is the designation for a true breeding and pure landrace strain. In most cases, the strain has lived in a remote area for several centuries and gone through countless generations to become uniform. These plants have also acclimated to the surrounding environment, and produce the specific oils, terpenes and compounds most important to survival in that area. When females of a *P1* are pollinated with males, the resulting seed progeny will produce an even crop of identical plants every year. The stability of a strain like this makes it a prime candidate for breeding.

F1 Hybrid

F1 is the designation for seed progeny produced by crossing two *P1* varieties to produce an even blending of the dominant traits of both strains. An *F1* is a very good plant for new growers, because it possesses a quality known as *hybrid vigor* which makes it grow with abandon, making it a much more trouble free plant for learning. An *F1* cannot be normally used for a cross, in order to avoid a phenotype breakdown resulting in many different-looking phenotypes in the progeny. The one exception to this rule is a cross to a P1 which would then be 50% of the genetic content of resulting progeny. Even then, there would be variation in the offspring.

F2 Hybrid

F2 is the designation for seed progeny where *F1* seeds are inbred, resulting in several dominant and sub-dominant traits showing themselves. It is impossible to predict which phenotypes will show within any given handful of seeds, so any ten seeds can be a mix of four or more phenotypes. Crossing out any desired phenotypes becomes an extremely complex process of selection from dozens or even hundreds of plants, making its use for breeding prohibitive.

F2 is also the designation of value in a succession of inbreeding crosses, where the breeder has a clear plan of action from beginning to end, with a specific result intended. In this context and F2 forms an integral part of genetic alignment, but is still seen as an intermediate cross possessing value, but unfinished. F2 indicates the process of a backcross, intended to reinforce some genes, while adding genetic variety or a desired trait to the result.

Several successive backcrosses, labeled as F2, F3, and F4 can bring the result to within a very fine margin of purity, stabilizing the genetic outcome and producing a true breeding hybrid strain with all the values of the original reinforced progeny. This needs to be done by a recognized expert, since the term F2 is subject to incorrect use.

The Dark side of F2 seeds:

Making F2 seeds has been a notorious practice of unscrupulous seed sellers who inbreed F1 hybrids, create knock-offs, rename them as popular named seeds and market them at a premium price with or without licensing or permission from the breeders. What happens in such a case, is an unraveling of the genetics contained in the F1, which will produce phenotypes representing the many traits of the progeny.

My opinion of F2 seeds has been to call them a 'mixed pack', since every plant in a pack of ten may be different from all the others. Although it is possible to glean a decent phenotype from these packs, unless you take clones from the mother plant you will never see it again. Because of the proliferation of unreliable Cannabis seed companies, buying an F2 can be a risky venture, and because of the nature of the existing seed industry, I personally do not recommend spending good money on F2 seeds, especially when accompanied by hyperbole.

The value of an F2 is at best debatable, at worst it is one of the many dark shames of the emerging Cannabis seed industry. Operating in a legal vacuum has made anything possible. Obviously no one is checking up.

Breeding and Crossing for Seed Progeny

The normal practice of growing usually entails identifying and destroying males in favor of female flower production. However, depending on the strain being grown, males can present an opportunity for the grower to perpetuate a pure strain to save seed, strengthen or bring out recessive genetic qualities within a cross, reinforce desirable dominant qualities, and collect genetics with the intention of creating ones own hybrid or stabilized strain.

Male 'African P1' + Female 'African P1' x Female 'African P1' + Male 'African P1'	**=**	**Offspring Progeny 'African P1'**

Crosses may be made at many different levels, and I'd like to discuss them as I describe crossing and stabilizing a strain, starting with the simplest, the familial pollination of a pure landrace strain which, when pollinated by its identical female kindred seed will produce a stable and identical seed every time. This strain will be named 'African P1. P1 is a common designation for a stably replicating land-race progeny seed in all seed-bearing plants.

Since the male and female of the landrace share genetics bred in from hundreds of years of isolation in its localized area, homogenization of the genetics has reached such uniformity that the resulting progeny can be said to be pure-breeding, and barring cross pollination with another gene pool will always carry the genetic traits of the original parent line. Landrace strains are extremely valuable for their inherent and stable traits; many P1 strains from the African continent are proving to be powerful medicine in the pursuit of cancer and human research. There is much we may yet learn from them, and good reason to preserve their genetics at all cost.

The next cross describes what is known as an F1 cross, where two stable purebred landraces are blended to produce an unstable but quite uniform hybrid in direct accordance with Mendel's law. The resulting 50/50 cross will possess an even blending of the characteristics of both parents, but the instability of the cross means a further cross (F2) of the ensuing seed will result in some variation.

Male 'Hawaiian P1' + Female 'African P1'	**=**	**Offspring Progeny 'Hawaiian/ African F1'**

An F1 cross also possesses something known as 'hybrid vigor': a fresh gene combination from two P1 plant causes the resulting offspring to be exceptionally vigorous in growth. It makes them easy to grow, and a highly suitable plant for gardeners new to Cannabis cultivation. The only direction an F1 can be crossed to avoid excessive genetic variation in the result is to backcross the progeny of one or the other of the P1 stock used in the production.

Stabilizing F1 seed progeny with a backcross requires slightly more planning than a basic F1 cross; it requires that you have saved the mother plant and cloned it in vegetation for a season in order to preserve the root of the cross, which always begins with a single mother plant. The F1 seed is collected and replanted to grow the following cycle or season. Simply flower all the resulting plants and select an appropriate male plant for the back cross, not to its sister plant, but instead to the original mother of the seeds produced.

50% Male 'Hawaiian'/ African P1' F1 + Female 'African P1'	**=**	**Offspring Progeny '75% African/ 25% Hawaiian'**

The combination of the 50/50 Hawaiian/African with the pure original female will result in a strengthening of the repeating genes, making the resulting genetic mix in this case 75% African and 25% Hawaiian.

The resulting seed will be closer to the original mother parent, showing most of the traits of the African, but some variation. The dominance of the African strain provides the first part of the name, and it is called African/Hawaiian. Selecting plants suited to further back crosses to the original mother becomes increasingly difficult, as many plants must be grown and examined for the traits of the parents, but such reinforcing of the genetics over several generations helps the strain become stable.

75% Male 'Hawaiian'/ 50 African F1 + Female 'African P1'	=	**Offspring Progeny '87.5% African/ 12.5% Hawaiian'**

From the resulting progeny, you must select plants bearing the same overall resemblance and traits as the original mother, and discarding all other phenotypes and traits, select a male to return its pollen to the root mother. The fourth back cross will yield 96.875 % purity on the side of the African phenotype, the resulting seed progeny will be ready for the final phase of stabilizing, where the original mother is now removed from the equation.

50% Male 'Hawaiian'/ African P1' F1 + Female 'African P1'	=	**Offspring Progeny '93.75% African/ 6.25% Hawaiian'**

There is certainly no law against a fifth or sixth backcross, which would achieve a purity of 96.875 and 98.4375 respectively. With a nearly 96% or greater genetic purity, the seeds may now be self-pollinated brother to sister to check for genetic consistency throughout the new strain. Naturally, every effort you make to purify and stabilize your seed-stock can only result in better medicinal Cannabis stock for the benefit of others, and personal seed collections help preserve and archive pure strains for others to breed with in the future.

Just this single line of crosses will generate an incredible amount of seeds which will need to be labeled and stored. Air tight containers can be kept in a freezer for many years, and every seeded plant can produce thousands of seeds!

Twenty or thirty thousand seeds and a thousand plants on hand for a breeder making a single line isn't a stretch; he would be typing males and females. The list of separate crosses for the line we just outlined can more easily be shown as:

Subject P1 progeny: Purebred African + Purebred Hawaiian

1. **African x Hawaiian = F1 hybrid (vigor)**
2. **African/Hawaiian x African P2 87.5%**
3. **African/Hawaiian x African P3 96.875%**
4. **African/Hawaiian x African P4 98.4375%**
5. **African/Hawaiian x African/Hawaiian sibling pollination**
6. **A-H-A Stable True Breeding Hybrid**

This cross was only a theoretic exercise, and did not take into account the hundreds of traits a Cannabis plant may have, nor the content or ratios of the four-hundred-and-twenty-one medical compounds contained in Cannabis that are now being sought by practitioners wishing to selectively enhance certain medical qualities inherent in them. It simply mathematically adds up the genetic content to estimate purity. Any genetic 'sports' that are created need to be discarded.

Now that we can use gas chromatography to identify strains containing these compounds, we may use this hard data to enhance these natural selective breeding techniques and take us in the right direction when seeking out the cancer-fighting compounds in those strains.

Let us say you acquired a fine cut (clone) from California, which is well known for its potency, and after trying it, you decide you want to save the genetics from the clone and preserve the genes in seed form. You can simply clone the mom, seed it with another type and use a series of back crosses to end up with a 98.4375% perfect replica.

Here is an example of a cross (still under way) from a San Fernando OG Kush clone, where I cross the clone to an F1 3-way hybrid, namely the male pollen of a White Widow / Mexican x Orange Diesel. Again, it is absolutely critical to back cross only to the original mother plant to systematically increase the percentage of presence of the desired genetics, in this case the OG. Once the genes have been chosen, they must be maintained, with no additional injection of genes from other strains. With each cross back to the original clone mother, Kush genes will be strengthened. From the initial cross, it will go like this:

Subject: Cross cloned genetics to preserve an SVG –OG cut

I was lucky enough to have been gifted with a clone from a very famous strain from California, the San Fernando Valley OG Kush. This strain is well known for its incredibly potent buds, and a distinct OG taste. A cut can be reproduced with most of its attributes intact by utilizing a series of back crosses of seed progeny to the mother cut, increasing the percentage of parent genes with each cross, in this case San Fernando Ocean Grown Kush.

7. **San Fernando Valley Ocean Grown (SFV-OG)**
8. **SFVOG Kush Clone X White Widow / Mexican x Orange Diesel (50% OG)**
9. **SFVOG x SFV/WW-MOD-I (75% SFV OG)**
10. **SFVOG x SFV/WW-MOD-II (87.5% SFV OG)**

11. **SFVOG x SFV/WW-MOD-III (96.875% SFV OG)**
12. **SFVOG x SFV/WW-MOD-IV (98.4375% SFV OG)**
13. **SFVOG x SFV/WW-MOD-V (99 %+) (Self cross)**

Result: "OGKK" 99.5% ± traits and characteristics to the original mother

If you were really fanatical about it, (who of us aren't?) an additional back cross from a male of the ***OGKK*** to the SFV-OG Clone could bring the strain to within a hair of pure (99.5% +) making it a true-breeding hybrid within less than 1% with all of the in-crossed genes blended in to the cross.

Left uncrossed, the new hybrid should produce offspring the same as a P1 landrace strain, creating uniform plants, predictable traits and crop results, and true-breeding seeds. As a stable hybrid, the new strain presents new opportunities for breeding, as it may now take the place of a P1 and be used in any cross.

As you can see, creating crosses and hybrids is quite a bit of work, and requires some careful planning and an end goal. Patience is key since it will take six or seven seasons or generations to reach the end of the project, but once created, the new hybrid has the value put into it by the breeder.

Reproducing seeds with the intention of archiving and saving and sharing with future generations is also a key benefit to back-engineering seeds from clone progeny into seed form or creating new hybrids. When done correctly, specific traits, resins and medicines may be saved and studied, and provide all of their medical benefits for generations of people well into the future.

The Super-Start Box

Even experienced growers face a challenge when starting seedlings, and the first week is absolutely critical. Follow these simple principles and you will be guaranteed solid sprouting, and prevent your seedlings from languishing and dying in the early stage of life.

The factors of light, space, air and water need to be properly balanced in order to effectively stimulate vigorous growth.

First, weak lighting will make seedling stems stretch, so I recommend your lights should be very bright and close to keep stems strong and help seedlings develop evenly. There are two ways to make the space brighter, you may add more lights, or you may make the space smaller. Warmth also coaxes the seed to sprout, so lighting should be close to the tops of the pots. CFL lighting makes this possible, being bright and relatively cool as well. Lights can be within four inches of the plant without burning them. Lighting for seedlings should be set to sixteen hours light and eight hours of dark for the first two to three weeks before moving to 12-1 schedule.

In the above photo, the upper wardrobe shelf space is twenty-one inches high by twenty-one inches deep by thirty-two inches wide, and lit with 700w (equivalent wattage) CFL lights (The actual power draw is 214w). The lights hang down nine inches from the top, and the pots were five inches tall. The lights in the wardrobe were just eight inches from the tops of the pots, and the warmth caused the seedlings to pop up in just two days.

Active and vigorous air flow is essential to the seedlings early cell growth, and Cannabis likes an active air flow during daytime and lighting hours. Especially important for seedlings, this airflow is used like an airfoil by the emerging leaves, catching it and bending the tender stem back and forth. This creates microscopic fissures in the stem tissues, which are repaired during the dark hours, and contribute to strengthening and stiffening the stems. In the wardrobe above a strong fan is placed on the shelf below the growing area, and directs the flow of air upwards through the gap next to the back wall.

Watering must be done actively, checking the pots daily for weight, and making sure they do not dry out. Flushing will be required at ten to twelve days since the growing environment accelerates the seedlings growth.

It is important that the roots be allowed to properly fill and surround the inside of the pot, first with your seedlings, and every time you pot up. This forms a series of root layers inside the root-ball, increasing the efficiency of the entire root system of your plants.

At around two weeks your seedlings will be ready to apply a thorough flush and a single application of a one-quarter strength solution of organic vegetation nutrients to promote new growth.

At seventeen days, these assorted seedlings have been hard at work. As evidenced by the pale color and slightly yellow leaf-tips, they suffered nutrient lock at about fourteen days and have now been flushed of heavy yellow sediments built up under the intense lighting.

The tight compression of light, space and airflow makes the seedlings progress at an accelerated pace, so basic plant management practices such as watering and flushing need to be more frequent.

At twenty-one days, your seedlings should be doing great. Stalks will be five to six sections high, opposite leaf arrangement, lots of primary fan leaves, and the cotyledon (first) and original 'blade' leaf will have withered. Depending on the strain type, seedlings may be from three to six inches tall, and branches will form at the base of the leaves.

At three weeks the plants will also be challenged for height. If they are tall and getting close to the lights lower the shelf to give them headroom. When you increase the space, increase the lighting as well, doubling the CFL wattage to compensate. (Increasing light is a recurring theme; larger plants need more and brighter lights to keep up with the vegetative growth.)

It is natural for the males to show maturity first, so watch for early indications of maturity by looking for alternating phylotaxy (arrangement of the growing leaves) and greater than average size and vigor. There is only so much light to go around, so removing the males will benefit the others from more available light in the space. Culling and removing the male plants is another way to increase the light in your space.

The roots of growing seedlings may be checked by gently flipping the plant upside down and carefully pulling the pot off the bottom to inspect the soil mass of the pot. If the growing roots are completely surrounding the outside of the soil next to the pot, you may select new larger pots, and pot up to prepare for full vegetative growth. If the roots aren't filling the pot, wait another week before proceeding.

Replant the seedlings into six-inch pots with fresh soil and expand your space by dropping the shelf to compensate for height, or by moving the growing plants into a larger vegetation space to provide more room and light to continue the next one-to-two months of growth and expansion. Once 12-1 lighting has been initiated, the seedlings will begin growing vigorously and fill their growing branches with new foliage, so be ready for them to begin taking on height and size very quickly from here on.

Cannabis plants may easily be held in vegetation state for many months or even years, and provide thousands of cuttings. A longer vegetation period will produce a larger plant, provide stronger cuttings and if it is simply flowered at full size, it will return a greater yield of buds as well.

A Micro-Grow Model

"Micro-grow" is the term used to describe a garden commonly done in a standard sized bedroom closet, growing just a few plants to a limited size. It is the common choice for many new growers, and works reasonably well for growing a small crop of four to six Cannabis plants.

Most closets are already painted white on the inside, and it makes a very good environmental capsule for growing some herb. A standard closet space will handle up to 600w of combination lighting and is pretty easy to set up without damage. A 2' x 4' x 6' closet will create a very nice miniature environment that you can control. Movable white walls allow you to expand the space, and reflect light within the space for the plants use.

A simple CFL hood (above) can be made out of white corrugated plastic, cut half way through to form the hinging section, with a normally wired 120 volt bathroom fixture mounted right in the middle. The flaps need to be long enough to hang below the rather long CFL bulbs. I traced the holes, and poked the four lamp bathroom fixture through the back of the hood.

Fertilizer schedule

Always flush pots well before each fertilizer application throughout the lives of your plants, (about every 4 weeks) and let the soil dry out normally for maximum nutrient uptake before applying fertilizers. Mix dosages according to product directions, and soak generously. Watch the leaves for paling leaf color which will indicate the soil is nearly depleted of food, most noticeably Nitrogen.

- **No fertilizers** are needed before two weeks. Seedlings have a stored energy supply contained in the seed pod to get the plant started, and there are enough natural nutrients in unfertilized soil to allow a good start. Watch for yellowing first leaves to indicate it's time.
- **First Fertilization: Organic Tomato Food (9-11-11)** this is my vegetation food of choice; it can be applied at a half strength dilution at around two to three weeks old or as soon as paleness or yellowing leaves are noted.
- **Second Fertilization: 50:50 Super Bloom Formula** (6-20-10) and Organic Tomato Food (9-11-11) applied full strength directed dilution every 4 weeks will carry the plant into fall with a strong framework and size.
- **Third Fertilization: Organic Super Bloom Formula** (6-20-10) Bat guano is applied three to four weeks into flower to boost bud size and sustain production. Apply full strength.
- **Supplemental Bloom: Bloom Booster (0-10-10)** Alaskan fish Fertilizer (non– smelly) provides flower enhancement and boosts bud weight in the latter weeks of bloom, seven and eight.
- **Molasses Flush:** used in concert with the Bloom Booster (0-10-10) one tsp in a gallon of water, supplements magnesium and a few sugars for bud size.
- **Myco-Rhyzome:** These fungi are naturally found in the soil surrounding all plants and are helpful to their healthy growth. A Powdered Myco-Rhizome soil additive is commercially available which may be added to water to infuse into the soil along with a normal organic fertilizing. Myco-Rhizae naturally has a symbiotic relationship with the root hairs, and is essential to good plant health.

Wardrobe Cabinet: This wardrobe is perfect for germinating seedlings under Compact Fluorescent Light inside the closet space like the one shown to the left.

Movable Wall System: Makeshift closet space above has been expanded to roughly 6 x 6 feet using whiteboards clipped together to form movable walls.

Plan your systems

To grow a comprehensive rotation system, you are going to need several spaces to grow in at once because of the differing lighting requirements between seedlings, cuttings, mature plants and flowering females. Each successive stage needs a corresponding increase in lumens to provide the plants with enough energy to grow up, increase mass and then flower. The formula below is great for a closet space or a little larger, increase lighting with increased square footage.

Seedlings and Cuttings: A small cupboard or wardrobe-sized space set to a sixteen-hour light cycle where the space can be shrunk to intensify four 150 watt CFL lights, dropping shelves allow the space to be expanded too allow for the seedling's increasing growth during the adolescent phases of growth. This can be used for rooting clones when you are ready to make clones from vegetative plants.

Mature Plants: A larger 'closet sized' space is needed for mature plants to grow in, with increased lighting to fill the space, and movable walls to compress or expand the size like the seedling space. This space can be multi-purpose space when flowering time comes. Vegetative light set to the 'photo periodic control 12-1 schedule. The hood shown opposite can easily hold ten 200w CFL lights, and easily support ten plants. A grow-hut works well in the summer too; check out my plans on page 65.

Flowering: You can switch the same growing area to flowering, or add another similar sized space for a fully functional growing system. Lighting hours are set to ten hours on and fourteen off for maximum response. A 400w high pressure sodium lamp can be added to the CFL lighting hood to increase the lumens dramatically, add in the red rays of the autumn cycle and provide fuller spectrum lighting for the plants greater health.

Growing your own

Many people who are now interested in growing Cannabis will only do so for their own use. The knowledge of its herbal efficacy is now widespread, and people who are educated about Cannabis will just do it. What follows is a simple plan using a closet-sized space, which is designed to maximize the yield of a miniature space, providing a steady personal supply for a patient's needs.

This schedule borrows from several different styles of growing and uses several different lighting schedules to complete the system; after several years of testing different methods to find the most effective method of personal growing, I designed this particular regimen to provide an easy method for the ordinary gardener to use.

The equipment is easy to obtain, and the methods below have been proven to work successfully. If you follow these schedules you can quickly and easily learn how to grow Cannabis, and provide yourself a continuous supply of medical grade Cannabis with the least possible expense.

A movable shelf in this wardrobe lets me 'squeeze' the space to keep the lighting close to the tops of the seedlings. The warm CFL's will coax the seedlings out of the soil, and as they reach toward the light, the shelf may be lowered to accommodate their increasing height.

Lighting schedules

Seedlings from germination to 2-3 weeks: can be lit under 16 hours of bright CFL light in a compressed space, (2 x 3 feet) three to six hundred watts CFL will only draw 168 watts overall. Keep the space small for warmth and to compress the intensity of the lights. A wardrobe cabinet works well as a starting space; keep a fan going in the bottom to properly circulate the air inside the cabinet.

Adolescent to Mature: The change from 16-8 to 12-1, and inner foliage growth takes off. 12-1 lighting will significantly shorten vegetation time due to the powerful vegetative response to resting periods. All the energy and nutrients the flowers need are stored in the plant and ready blast it into bloom – and it does! Pistils will show in one to three days.

Above and below, the same hood with and without HPS lighting added.

Flowering Frenzy: The change from 12-1 to 10-14 lighting is a very easy one for the plants, and the well rested plants respond immediately with an explosion of pistils. All the energy and nutrients the flowers need are stored in the plant and ready blast it into bloom; and it does! Pistils will show in one to three days.Using ten hours of light and fourteen hours darkness has several advantages. Plants will stretch less and having made more growth on the branches, produce more flowers and finish earlier. 10-14 sharply decreases leaf production, diverting energy instead to making flowers and resin, resulting in smoother smoking Cannabis that is all flowers and no harsh smoking leaf.

10-14 lighting has the added advantage of making it possible to cycle time-dated plants through a few at a time, providing a steady supply every few weeks.

Add a 400w HPS to your CFLS hood to increase the light again, and add the fall spectrum of light to your grow to finish up the buds to 8 weeks and beyond. Note that I increase the lighting each time I change schedules.

Your experience will provide precise information on the ideal length of flowering required for the strains you are growing, but bear in mind many strains will finish a week early under this schedule. Use the Journal to take notes, knowledge is power!

Lights on in flower: The eerie yellow glow of the HPS provides red spectrums needed to enhance and complete the flowering period of Cannabis.

All CFL? Yes it CAN be done. This NYC Diesel bud was grown under CFL Lighting. The plants grow normally and healthy, but the buds produced are very small.

Combining light schedules for rotating crops

Caregivers who need to grow to provide a continuous supply to patients will have to plan rotating crops to produce the required prescribed strains, so keeping seedlings, clones, vegetative and flowering plants all at the same time will become necessary.

This can require three or four spaces, each with differently timed cycles. Not all of the strains in a caregivers garden will grow the same size or finish at the same rate, and so overlapping time schedules and plant size during the course of the season can easily become a challenge of space and light management.

In such a system, the diminishing lighting schedule is not as practical, so instead an alternate short production schedule for flowering like the 10-14 can be used, which also reduces production costs.

Tagging each plant with the entry date to the flowering room and the strain's estimated finish time will identify when plants are ready to finish. This way, plants coming from vegetative room under the 12-1 can be easily rotated to the flower room. Plants flowered this way will respond well to the sudden drop in light duration and very quickly go into bloom.

Building Strong Roots

The roots are the foundation of the plant's growth. They grow and branch very much like the upper half of the plant, and when restricted will form strong lattices of roots surrounding the outside of the pots, a condition known as "root-bound." This is a gauge you may use to the greater advantage of your plant's health, by allowing the roots to circle the pots before potting up to the next size.

When growing seedlings, a strong start is needed, so the growth of strong roots depends on their ability to create a strong system. Start seeds in a half-pot of soil, limiting the growing medium. Two-inch pots are well suited to the tiny set of roots coming from a fresh seed, and allow it to fill the medium quickly.

Seedlings will easily live two weeks to a month in this small amount of soil, provided flushing is accelerated, and the soil is maintained at a moist enough level. Roots should be going strong and ready at around three to four weeks.

Allow the seedling's roots to fill the half-pot and wrap around the sides before topping the soil up to the cotyledons with fresh soil.

Allow pots to dry out, and place the root-ball on top of the fresh soil, press gently down to slightly break the soil, and water in thoroughly. Two weeks later, they should have filled the pots again, and be ready for the next phase, potting up. As the plants gain in size, this process will accelerate, so keep as close an eye on the roots as you do the rest of the plant.

The first section of stem from the root to the cotyledon is composed of very special tissues which when buried will produce an additional flush of roots, which strengthen and anchor the plant as it grows taller.

You can see the potential root nodes as small whitened bumps on the stem. The seedlings may be buried up to the cotyledon as soon as sufficient height has been reached.

When sizing up your pots, only pot up an inch at a time, so as to continue to restrict root growth and make a strong root-ball.

Use the square pot's shape to maximize the new growing area by placing the corners of the root-ball to point to the flat sides of the new pot as shown.

Start with a small handful of soil in the bottom of the pot to allow for downward as well as side root growth, and place the root-ball on top. Fill in the corners, pressing down gently to avoid air pockets being formed, then add soil to the top, and bury as much of the first stem section as necessary with each potting.

Finish with a solid watering to equalize the moisture of the new pot, and apply the first full strength feeding with your vegetation formula tomato food fertilizer.

The plants will go into an immediate stage of growth, and begin to really increase mass. With a solid foundation in the roots, they may now be slowed by potting to larger pots before flowering.

Clone Propagation

Cloning your females is an efficient method to propagate. The maturing seedlings can take two months to complete, and using cuttings will cut the next crop production time by half. Replicating your existing plants for repeated crops of symptom specific medicine is a real advantage for anyone who uses Cannabis for treatment.

A basic rooting powder will do fine for Cannabis cuttings, I prefer a **#4 rooting powder.** ***Indole-3-acetic acid*** has been in use for decades and is a known and trusted rooting agent.

Rockwool cubes make a good sterile medium for the roots, although cuts can be rooted right in soil for the experienced.

Once your plants have reached maturity and sex is determined, there will be a lot of inside and lower woody branches and foliage which tends to sap the energy away from the growing terminal and branch buds if they are left to grow.

These secondary branches should be removed anyway as part of your program to keep the plants bug free, promote the plant's health, and direct energy to the growing buds.

I select the largest of the branches between 2 and 3 inches long with the terminal from the lower center stem, but any of the smaller branches with a terminal will make good cuttings given additional growing time.

Use a razor knife and slice the branch off right at its base and place directly into water. If there is a burl or bump at the base of the stem, take it with the cutting. It will look like a disc on the end of the cut, and include the cambium layer 'wood' to increase the chances of successful rooting.

1. **Label and presoak rock-wool cubes and shake out the excess water.**
2. **Shake some rooting powder onto a saucer for dipping. Keep the container sealed, and discard any excess when finished.**
3. **Take the cutting from the water and scrape the side of the cutting gently to expose the cambium layer which will produce roots.**
4. **Dip the cut end of the clone in the powder and lightly tap to remove the excess.**
5. **Stick the end into the hole in the cube, and place in the domed humidity tray, covering immediately.**
6. **Once your cuts are all made, keep the cubes together in blocks so they won't lose humidity too quickly.**
7. **Clip the largest leaves to square ends to halt excessive transpiration and focus the clone on making roots.**

Check your clone chamber often, and open the dome daily to allow fresh air inside for the plants to breathe. Fanning the plants for a few seconds is a good practice; it will move the stagnant air nearest the leaves out and allow fresh air to replace it. Even under a dome, the cuttings continue to process gases while making roots.

Sexing: Placing clones in water in a dark place for several days will allow hormones to build up enough in the cuts to show sex.. This technique can be used to sex the seedlings before removing the males.

Cubed cuttings under a single 40w CFL light, inside a domed humidity tray until roots show out the bottom.

One root pops out the end, while its sister has yet to show. Roots will poke out the bottom of the cube starting in 5-7 days.

Cuttings should start producing roots in five to seven days. The new clones will quickly produce a nice explosion of roots under the right conditions, and they can be planted into soil as soon as there are roots popping out the bottom of the cubes.

Square pots are great for saving space, since they take up much less space than round pots, and they fit together in a block. They are also easy to use during potting up.

The same cutting a few days later. Secondary rootlets form quickly, and the dying yellowing root may be trimmed with a razor blade.

Clones will grow a pot full of roots quickly, so these three inch pots are larger than the ones used for seedlings.

10 days older, and growing strong with some food. Even at this size, a clone is fully mature, and can be flowered immediately.

Fill your three-inch pots to within an inch of the top with fresh soil, and place the cube with its clone in the center, with the corners pointing to the sides of the pot. This leaves large triangular corner spaces that are easy to fill in with soil. Press the soil into the corners and fill so the top of the rooting cubes are covered and the soil is in contact with the clone. Planting corner to side is good practice anytime you are potting your plants to the next size up. It effectively eliminates air pockets and dry spots in the soil which may desiccate roots and adversely affect all of the plants systems.

Soak the soil immediately to encourage roots to fill the pot, and place your clones under bright CFL light and active air movement to stimulate growth. Allow a few days to a week to settle in and fertilize with the 'Tomato Food' (9-11-11) at half the directed strength.

As soon as the roots take hold and begin drawing nutrients from the soil they will search the pot for nutrients, filling it and circling the outside of the pot. Strong growth should be almost immediate.

After about two weeks, the clones should fill the pots with roots, and be ready to pot up to six-inch square pots. Carefully flush each plant, pot up to the next size, and reapply nutrients. Use full strength vegetative formula to fully initiate plant growth.

Flush your plants well prior to every increase in pot size, use good watering practices to flush out soil build-up.

Clones may easily grow to sixteen inches tall in a six-inch square pot before needing final repotting, in just a few more weeks. Three to five gallons are great for final pots. Use tomato food to keep them in vegetative stage, and just before you switch to flowering light, flush again and change your nutrients to super bloom to encourage plants to show sex. Take cuttings before the plant is in full flower, and begin the cloning process all over. With time you will automatically know how many clones to cut to grow the next crop, so take more than you need, to allow for mortality until you are proficient. Share your extra cuttings with your friends! A connoisseur's cut makes a great gift!

Nurserymen refer to the 'drip line' (the distance from the plant where water droplets run off from the outermost leaves) as a guide to determine the outside edge of the pot, when they pot up to larger containers.

Troubleshooting

Most of the problems associated with growing Cannabis stem from the use of containers. My most common question to growers experiencing trouble is whether the pots have been recently flushed to remove accumulated sediments. Returning the soil to baseline can allow pH to be corrected and de-stress the roots and plant systems.

Close observation of the leaves, stems and general plant growth will give you clues as to what is going on in the inner parts of the plant. If your plants are having problems, check the list below. My most common advice to resolve problems includes flushing the container to remove wastes and return the soil to near baseline conditions.

Fertilizer burn and nutrient lock up can crisp the leaves.

Symptoms and solutions

Nitrogen (N) deficiency: Leaves are a uniform yellow or light green; leaves die & drop; growth is slow.

Magnesium (Mg) deficiency: Margins of the leaves are turned up, and the tips may be twisted. Leaves are yellowing (and may turn brown), but the veins remain green.

Potassium (K) deficiency: Leaves are browning or yellowing. Necrotic patches, especially around the edges of the leaf, which may be curled. Plant may tend to stretch.

Phosphorous (P) deficiency: Leaves are dark green or red/purple. Stems and petioles may have purple & red on them. Leaves may turn yellow or curl under. Leaf may drop easily. Growth may be slow and leaves may be small.

Copper (Cu) deficiency: Plants won't flower, even though they get 12 hours of darkness for over 2 weeks. The night period is not completely dark, or there is too much nitrogen. Flush and use a Super Bloom formula.

Iron (Fe) deficiency: Leaves are yellow or white, but the veins are mostly green.

Manganese (Mn) deficiency: Leaves are light green or yellow beginning at the base, while the leaf margins remain green. Dead spots are found between veins.

Zinc (Zn) deficiency: Leaves are twisted.

Over-fertilization (especially Nitrogen): Tips of leaves are yellow, brown, or dead, plants otherwise looks healthy. Leaves curled under and look like a claw, and are dark green.

Over-watering: Stems may be soft. Gray, brown, or gold and many leaves are crispy. Damaged roots, or insufficient soil aeration (Repot, add sand or Perlite)

The plant is wilted, even though the soil is moist: Over-fertilization, soggy soil, damaged roots, disease.

Leaves twist, then turn brown or die: The lights are too close to the plant, or very rarely, a Calcium (Ca) or Boron deficiency.

A light green color shows these plants need nitrogen soon or they will begin to shed foliage and die.

Leaf edge curling indicates a magnesium deficiency in the plant.

Iron: Fe is not available to plants when the pH of the water or soil is too high. If deficient, lower the pH to about 6.5 (for Rockwool, about 5.7), and check that you're not adding too much P, which can lock up Fe. Read your fertilizer's ingredients to see that it contains nutrients that are chelated for maximum uptake availability. – Chelated iron might read something like "Iron EDTA."

Zn, Fe, and Mn: These deficiencies often occur together, and are usually from a high pH.

PH factor: The pH of water after adding any nutrients should be around 5.9-6.5 (in Rockwool, 5.5-6.1). Generally speaking, the micro-nutrients (Fe, Zn, Mn, Cu) get locked out due to high pH (alkaline) above 7.0, while the major nutrients (N, P, K, Mg) can be less available in acidic soil or water (below 5.0). Lowering the pH is simple using a flush if that's the problem, so the nutrients may once again become available. Tap water can be too alkaline. Soils with lots of peat or other organic matter in them tend to get too acidic, which some dolomite lime will help to fix.

Many factors can change the actual level of nutrients the plants will need. Certain nutrients are "invisible" to TDS meters, especially organics, so use TDS level only as an estimate of actual nutrient levels. When in doubt about a new fertilizer, follow the fertilizer's directions for feeding tomatoes. Grow a few tomato or radish plants nearby for comparison. A pH meter is an excellent investment in your plant's happiness.

Check your water

Crusty faucets and shower heads mean your water is "hard," due to too many minerals. Tap water with a TDS (total dissolved solids) level of more than around 200ppm (parts per million) is "hard" and should be looked into, especially if your plants have a chronic problem. Ask your water company for an analysis listing, which will usually list the pH, TDS, and mineral levels (as well as the pollutants, carcinogens, etc) for the tap water in your area.

Regular water filters will not reduce a high TDS level, but the costlier reverse osmosis units, distillers, and de-ionizers will. A digital TDS (Total Dissolved Solids) meter (or EC = electrical conductivity meter) is an incredibly useful tool for monitoring the nutrient levels of nutrient solution, and will pay for itself before you know it.

Check the pH often, and flush only when necessary. Plant excretions can make soil trend toward acid if not properly managed, so watch for yellow runoff when watering. With soil, pH can be managed with proper watering and flushing techniques.

Final week of flowering taper off to plain water. Many factors can change the actual level of nutrients the plants will need. Certain nutrients are "invisible" to TDS meters, especially organics, so use TDS level only as an estimate of actual nutrient levels. When in doubt about a new fertilizer, follow the fertilizer's directions for feeding tomatoes. Grow a few tomato or radish plants nearby for comparison.

Cold – Cold weather (below 50F/10C) can lock up phosphorous. Some varieties, especially equatorial Sativas don't take well to cold weather. If you can keep the roots warmer the plant will be able to take cooler temps than it otherwise could.

Over-watered above, below just right.

Curved fan leaves: too much Nitrogen in flower!

Clones – yellowing leaves on un-rooted clones can result from too much light, or the stem may not be firmly touching the rooting medium. Turn off any CO_2 until they root. Too much fertilizer can shrivel or wilt clones – plain tap water is fine.

Powder Mildew – A humid grow-room is also prime breeding for powdery mildew. Managing humidity and air circulation is key to prevention, but plants may be treated for powder mildew with a foliar spray of milk on all upper and lower leaf surfaces.. Be sure to cover the soil surface when spraying to prevent it affecting the soils Mycorrhiza population.

Heat – If the lights are too close to the plant, the tops may be curled, dry, and look burnt, mimicking a nutrient problem. Your hand should not feel hot after holding it for a minute at the top of the plants. Raise the lights and/or aim a fan at the hot zone. Room temps should be kept under 85F (29C).

Humidity – Thin, shriveled leaves can result from low humidity. 40-80 % is usually fine. Mold and fungus - Dark patchy areas on leaves and buds can be mold. Lower the humidity and increase the ventilation if mold is a problem. Remove any dead leaves, wherever they are. Keep your garden clean.

Insects – White spots on the tops of leaves can mean spider mites underneath.

Sprays – Foliar sprays can have a lens effect under bright lights, causing small white, yellow or burnt spots which can be confused with a nutrient problem. Some sprays can also cause chemical reactions.

Insufficient light – tall, stretching plants are usually caused by too much distance between the light and the plant, or using the wrong kind of light. Don't use regular incandescent bulbs or halogens to grow Cannabis. Invest in fluorescent lighting (good) or HID lighting (much better) which supply the high-intensity light that Cannabis needs for good growth and tight buds. Even better, grow in sunlight.

Low light is causing this plant to stretch

Spider Mites

Spider Mites (*Tetranychidae*) are actually spiders with eight legs and small, whip-like mouthparts uniquely designed for ingesting plant sap. They are a common and pernicious greenhouse pest which, once established, can be difficult to eradicate.

Spider mites can be brought into a mite-free home from outside in the garden by pets or while you are working with other garden plants, they may come from plants bought at a nursery, or migrate from your existing house plants. Spider can wreak havoc on your environmental capsule.

Watch for pinpoint-sized yellow spots on the leaves (stippling). and then you'll find these characters on the lower side of the leaves. They are very tiny, but under a magnifying glass you can see three stages:

1. ***Egg*** (tiny yellow clusters next to the center leaf-vein)
2. ***Larval*** (a small dark dot, not moving)
3. ***Adult*** (larger dot with legs, lays eggs, runs around eating!)

Misting this plant **has revealed a severe infestation of the most dreaded of the garden pests, Spider mites (Tetranychidae).**

You can see the webs easily when you mist the plants *(above)*. The earlier you identify and eradicate them, the better for you and your garden. If the mites get out of control, they can be very difficult to get rid of. Practicing prevention is the key, cleaning tools and hands, and keeping the area swept up at all times, and wearing clean clothing.

Here is a means of effective pesticide-free removal. Set a hose on a low pressure, or using a constant flow sprayer, set the nozzle to semi-coarse spray. Leaning it over, hose the plant down from the underside of the leaves. This will physically remove the mites, carrying them off the plants and down the drain, which is where they belong!! Be ready to stake them up until the weight of the water has flown off and they can stand up on their own. Repeat every few days to get the hatched mites left behind, or the infestation can recur. (Careful, too often and it leaches Nitrogen from the leaves.)

Certain insecticides will work well in combination with this showering technique. Neem Oil derivatives perform a dual purpose, providing a 'tonic' for plant health but should only be used in the vegetative stage of growth. Many patients and growers, having tried the Neem oil products have noted that it leaves an unpleasant flavor behind if it is used too late in the plant's development. Neem oil should be avoided during flowering entirely.

Close-up next to golden trichomes: **Full grown females may lay 20 eggs a day and live 3 to 4 weeks.**

Mites warm themselves in the lights: **By the time you can see this many on the upper surface of the fan leaves, you already have a severe infestation in progress.**

Nathan Dodson's Spider Mite Hell

This recipe is particularly nasty to the bugs, while doing no harm whatsoever to the plants. It can be used right up to harvest, and is a completely natural homemade recipe with no deadly residues.

Take a half dozen habanero peppers, dice well and do not discard seeds. Mix into about 3 cups of water and keep it under a boil. Keep it stewing for about 20 to 30 minutes, strain pepper material and dilute into a water boil. It doesn't affect overall taste and severely burns the mites to death. It's kind of like a caustic acid, without harmful side effects.

Caution! Use proper ventilation and eye protection when brewing this to avoid severe eye irritation.

Dawn Peterson Smith's Spider Mite Death

This spray combines the toxicity (only to mites) and the smothering effect of Neem, without the lingering aftertaste, which many smokers find unpleasant. This recipe may be used up to halfway through bloom.

- **One tsp Sesame Oil**
- **One tsp Lecithin**
- **One quart water**

This recipe couldn't be simpler: Put all into blender and mix thoroughly. Sesame oil is deadly to spider mites and won't impart the taste that Neem might, making it perfect to use.

Trimming Foliage

Throughout the plant's life it will grow and discard leaves naturally. Any leaves that yellow, wither, or become damaged may be removed for the sake of the plant's health. Since damaged leaves can't be repaired and will naturally die anyway, and leaving them on may present an opportunity for mold or mildew to grow, or other complications to develop.

Simple plant maintenance and time spent with the plants allows us to observe that the first and oldest leaves will complete their life cycle first. Any leaf trimming always begins with the oldest leaves on the plant, and leaves behind the newest growth, which is then boosted by the redistribution of the plant's energy and ultimately assists in its bud production.

"Leafing" is a simple technique done in the late vegetative cycle of the plant. At around six to eight weeks of vegetation the plant is starting to throw off early leaves that have finished, and some of the growing inner foliage that tends to prevent light from reaching the center of the plant will be yellow from light deprivation. You may notice reddening on the leaf stems; this is also a good indicator that the leaf is nearing the end of its useful time.

- Primary leaves located on the stem at the base of each branch.
- Secondary leaves at the base of each of the branch nodes.
- Secondary leaves on the branch nodes that point toward the plant's center which shade the inside.
- Best trim has the most trichomes on it, and is preferred for making top grade medicines.

Any of these leaves can be removed in preparation for the oncoming fall lighting. Trimming has several benefits, physically removing leaves can help to lower onboard nitrogen content, it allows light to penetrate and helps control the movement of pests, and most importantly, redistributes energy so the nodes and branches left grow larger flowers. Take a systematic approach, and work from large to smallest, taking several passes over the plant so that leaf grades may be saved separately for use in making oils of various types, for juicing, or extracting tinctures for cannabis medicines and salves. You're going to appreciate having these extra materials saved when you are able to help a friend or family member with some much needed medicine.

Maturation and the Vegetation Stage

During seedling and adolescent phases of growth (one to four weeks) branches and leaves forming at the nodes will appear at opposite sides on the stem starting when the cotyledon opens and the first leaves appear. They open and separate for the second pair to form and emerge, opposite the first pair.

The primary leaf pairs will form at ninety degrees to one another during adolescent phase, starting with a single blade, then three, and five as each pair emerges, and the size and strength of the stem increases. The blades are odd-numbered, with as many as thirteen blades on some of the primary (fan) leaves.

Nodes will emerge along with the leaves, forming at the base of each primary leaf, which eventually form the primary branches, along which will grow more leaves and alternating nodes.

At around four to six weeks, the primary leaf and branch growth phyllotaxy will show a marked change in growth pattern, forming leaf and branch nodes in an alternating pattern starting at the tips of all the growing terminals and continuing through flowering. Upon reaching maturity, the plants will branch outward and increase size and weight with additional leaf and branch nodes forming along the lengthening branches.

Often the males may outgrow the females, and the dominant plants may be mistaken for a female by the novice grower. The overall stature of the males will often be slightly more vigorous than the smaller females; this is by design, to maximize pollen distribution to as many females as possible.

Careful inspection and testing is recommended, to ensure that mistakes are not made when selecting females and males.

Cannabis must have the female flower fertilized in order to produce seed progeny. For every pistil that grows, an ovum in the flower bud prepares to be pollinated by a single grain of pollen. The pistil catches the pollen and microscopic cilia hairs guide the pollen grain as it slides it down into the ovum to become the new seed. Upon pollination, each of the pistils wither quickly since one grain does the trick.

For the purpose of producing sinsimilla (seed free) female flower buds, males are identified and removed as soon as their sex becomes apparent. If you decide to make seed, males can be sequestered and their pollen saved for later to pollinate a branch or a single selected female.

The Cannabis plant is naturally symmetrical, and with no trimming at all, most will eventually grow to form a classic 'Christmas Tree' shape.

Flowering Stage

The bloom schedule

A full understanding of vegetation and flowering is necessary when you are attempting to grow Cannabis, and it is best to try to recreate the conditions found in the environment. Simply stated, advancing darkness allows the photosensitive hormones in Cannabis leaves to build up in the fall, the resulting hormonal change signals it is time to bloom. Cannabis is a short-day flowering plant, which by definition needs 11 hours or less of light to correctly induce blooming.

A flowering schedule of twelve hours on and twelve off will not adequately provide the naturally increasing hormonal buildup caused by the diminishing hours of the autumn sun. The plant remains in semi-vegetative state, only producing moderate amounts of resin and flowers. Using this method, floral hormones build up more slowly, and vegetation slows, but does not stop, so finished weight contains more vegetation. Twelve hours on and twelve off is just barely enough dark period sufficient to flower and finish, and not enough to fully maximize the plants flowering potential.

Diminishing fall lighting is used to simulate the decreasing hours of light of the autumn as it occurs in nature, and is quite easy to implement in your grow. To begin using the Diminishing light technique, simply remove the interruption hour, and drop the lighting time to eleven and one half hours.

This allows floral hormones to build up and immediately begin producing flowers. The lighted period can then be to reduced in half-hour increments starting at eleven hours light and thirteen hours dark and reducing by a half-hour each week for the remaining weeks, finishing up in the final week with nine hours of light and fifteen hours of darkness.

Short period flowering

Drop the lighting severely from vegetation stage directly to ten hours of light and fourteen hours of darkness to induce flowering. The plants are given an incredibly fast buildup of hormones, and violently explode into bloom. When this shortened lighting schedule is used with the twelve and one schedule, it is perfect for providers who grow for the needs of many patients, since plants may be tagged with entry dates, rotated from a vegetating to a flowering environment and checked for ripeness according to specific growing and harvest-time requirements.

Conclusions

Combining multiple lighting techniques such as CFL lighting during seedling phase, the Photo Periodic Control during vegetative growth and finishing with the Diminishing fall Lighting or a Short Light Schedule is great for your plants' health, but the benefits don't stop there.

1. Power consumption for the duration of the project can be as little as one-half of normal, making micro-sized grows much more affordable for the hobby grower.
2. Low power usage and short schedules provide some stealth from nosey authorities.
3. Plant size, vigor, and yield are improved over the standard grow, and vegetation cycle may be shortened by as much as 2 weeks allowing an additional harvest each year.
4. Plants use fewer nutrients more efficiently.
5. Clone burnout is avoided by ending overexposure to light.
6. Plants finish with more flower weight and less trimming is required.

Circadian Rhythms

Every Cannabis strain will flower best using a schedule that best suits their naturally occurring rhythms. Depending on the strain, certain plants may flower best at specific light lengths below 10 hours of light or less.

Finding this 'sweet spot' is simply a matter of observing the strain as you diminish the light over successive cloned grows to discover which light length works best. This is generally found to be somewhere below ten hours of light, and the exact duration can be slightly different for each strain depending where they are from.

Once you have found the ideal lighting time, plants of this strain will react with explosive flowering, and can subsequently go straight to this time schedule to be finished.

Medical Cannabis growing is conceptually different from commercial growing. Its techniques are designed to nurture the health of the plant, and ensure healthier and happier plants, increasing both yield and potency.

The illness-fighting compounds known as Cannabinoids express themselves best in a fully healthy and vital plant, so naturally Cannabis grown with the best techniques will target specific medical conditions with the greatest possible success.

Harvesting

Trichomes and Ripeness

Near the end of the prescribed time for the strain you are growing, *(typically eight weeks for the average Indica)* you may start to check the trichomes for ripeness before you consider taking a harvest. Early in the buds' development, the oils on the ends of the capitate trichomes will be clear, (as shown right) and if sampled will produce a very uplifting effect, though it may not be long-lasting like the riper buds. Even an Indica can have a soaring effect similar to a sativa if the timing of the harvest is carefully placed in the early window. Yield tends to be less since the final few weeks are the time when the most bud weight is put on in terms of resin production. Certain terminals may even be selected for early harvest, allowing the rest to finish together.

With more time, the trichomes on the bud will turn cloudy as they become engorged with resin and swell up. Typically it is time to harvest the ripe buds. Testing for effects is again recommended, and it is also common practice to leave a plant for a late harvest test, when the trichomes begin to turn golden in color, and produce a more narcotic effect.

Comparing buds from each of the three phases of harvest will help you zero in on the most desirable medicinal results and allow you to target symptomatic relief by varying the effects of buds according to the type and severity of the condition.

Capitate trichomes are the glands through which the plant secretes sticky protective resins. Oil oozes out and forms a bulb on a clear stalk. It's always good to sample during different phases to discover which effect is most preferable for your needs or symptoms.

Trichomes

Checking trichome ripeness with a digital camera

This is a great idea for soon-to-be old farts like me. I'm in my fifties, and I have noticed that even after I got multi-focal lenses, I still wasn't really able to properly inspect the buds and trichomes for ripeness the way I used to. It seems my range of focus has changed some, so whether I like it or not, I must resign eventually to old age.

Thank goodness for modern digital photography! Advanced features like digital zoom, super macro, variable exposure, and timed release on digital cameras has made it very easy for anyone to set up and take high quality pictures with inspection for ripeness in mind. Many digital cameras are even fully automatic, simply point and shoot.

When you are shooting for macro clarity, set your camera on a tripod, still the fans in the room, and preferably shoot with the lights behind you. Sodium lights cause the yellow glow you will see in some of my pictures here. For the best color and resolution, shooting is best done under Metal halide.

Try a few experiments with distance but to get a decent trichome shot, place the camera two to four inches from the subject and shoot a frame. If it is out of focus, try a little zoom, or move the camera position and try again. I often poke my camera to within an inch of the subject or less, as shown above.

When you are getting a good shot set the delay timer so you can press the shutter and step back from the shot. This will allow the camera to be as still as possible when the picture is taken. I love shooting my plants, and I do it a lot. What's nice about digital images is that you can eventually go through and cull the files on your computer and voila! You have more memory!

I probably get one or two good shots I like out of every twenty I take, so don't worry, it is a numbers game, and the more that you do it the better you get. It is just lucky that it turned out to be a handy tool for old men too.

Curing and Storage

The Phased Harvest

When you examine the flowers on your nearly finished plant, you will see they are of varying ripeness. The outermost buds will naturally be done first, while the inside flowers may still be developing. A multi-phase harvest can help you get more total weight from each plant you grow by taking ripe buds first and allowing smaller buds to finish maturing.

The buds on the ends of the branches and the top colas will have been closest to the lighting, and absorbed more light, so all the plant's terminal flowers will have had the most energy directed to their growth by the plant. Taking these ripe buds first will redirect the plants energy to the unfinished buds, which will plump up and boost your harvest weight.

Optionally, you can harvest and store ripe and unripe buds separately. Riper buds have a heavier effect, while younger buds tend to provide a more uplifting experience when smoked. With the flowers categorized in this way, the connoisseur may then select his buds with these effects in mind, selecting more mature buds for pain, and less ripe ones for depression due to their uplifting effects.

Grading Trim Waste: When you are doing your trimming you will want to consider using every part of this medicinal marvel in a true value-added program to get the most out of the plants that you are growing with so much care and dedication. Trimming is often done when the buds are still wet, especially with a larger harvest. Turgid leaves are easy to trim, and graded trim can be used for value-added products like hash, edibles or oils.

The various sizes of leaves have more or less of the various compounds in Cannabis, and they are each useful. When trimming, care should be taken to separate each grade of material. Large paper grocery bags work well for grading and drying trim without the worry of mold occurring. Work from the largest leaves to the smallest like a production line, making sure to take the entire stem off the plant with the leaves.

Sweating to bleach leaf material: Cannabis can be treated with 'sweating' to bleach the chlorophyll from the leaves, and give it a golden color. Place the fresh leaves in black plastic bags, and leave it in a hot place so the moisture evaporates and condenses on the materials inside. The leaf inside will turn yellow in a few of days, neutralizing and bleaching all of the chlorophyll out of the materials. This helps to avoid the green taste and color in the end product when medical compounds are extracted. This can give the buds a beautiful golden color reminiscent of strains such as Colombian Gold. Move sweated buds on to the hanging and curing phase.

Try this in small batches to test your efforts before committing an entire crop to sweating. Sweating was common in the 1970's on Cannabis plantations in Central America where farmers would harvest entire fields at once.

Freeze drying: This works better for the smaller secondary leaves and bud trim, because it helps preserve the live oils and trichomes prior to processing into butter, hash or oil. The heat in the sweating process can also evaporate liquid oils on the smaller leaves, making it unsuitable for higher potency trim.

Trimming Method

- **Fan Leaves:** First, remove the largest of the leaves attached directly to the stems and branches. They are used for making CBD medicinal oils, or may be juiced fresh in a blender as a health supplement.
- **Secondary Leaves:** the leaves attached to the buds and surrounding the bud clusters often have plenty of trichomes on them, and are excellent for making Cannabis butter which may be added to all kinds of medicated sweet treats or 'medibles'.
- **Bud Trim:** Trimmed from around the buds during final bud manicuring, this is the very best of the trim, and chock full of trichomes and liquid oils dripping off the buds. It's the primo material for making hash and kif as well as premium potency Cannabis butter or hash oil.
- **Stems and sticks:** all the stems contain some oils which may be rinsed off with alcohol, and the fibres of the stems may be made into paper, or even distilled into fuel or alcohol before being composted.
- **Roots:** can be added to help improve your home compost piles. They add fibre, allow aeration, and improve compost quality

Drying buds: Once the buds have been properly trimmed and manicured, hang the branches on wires or strings in a cool, dark, curing chamber equipped with a circulating fan for at least a day or two so they won't dry out too fast right away.

Keep the temps low and on the third day, remove the buds by clipping them from the branches, and weigh to check for moisture content. Finished harvest weight may be estimated quite easily by weighing a marked sample branch while it is wet and testing its weight daily.

Begin the curing process when the buds reach 30% of wet weight. Check daily for the first week, squeezing one gently to check for firmness. They will seem spongy and moist at first, and then as they dry they will stiffen up on the outsides like small sugar candies.

Curing: This final process enhances and deepens the naturally occurring flavors of all the Cannabinoid compounds. The buds lose their green taste and take on the more complex flavors of the oils, flavinoids and THC compounds in the buds.

- Loosely pack the buds into glass jars, about two thirds full, and seal for a full day. This will allow the humidity in the jar to equalize, so that the buds re-soften.
- Open the jars and let them sit with the lids open for an hour to let the humid air from the buds in the jar escape, and note the buds stiffening again slightly before you reseal for another day.
- Repeat until buds remain stiff, then seal permanently and store jars in a cool and dark place.

Long-term storage: When kept in a controlled environment such as a basement or cellar, the preserved buds will store well and continue to cure for as long as they are sealed. Exposure to light and heat will degrade potency more than any other factor.

Butter and Baking

Cannabis resins are very easily extracted using butter to capture the oils. Top-grade trim clipped from the buds can be a valuable resource, expanding the usefulness of your entire crop's output.

It's an easy recipe. All you need is a pound of butter to an ounce of freeze-dried bud trim, a one or two gallon cooking pot of water and some cheesecloth to extract the oils in your trim to butter. Using the method below, you will easily extract the oils from the trim, and completely avoid any plant material in your end product.

How to Make Canna Butter

1. **Fold your cheese-cloth so that it is four layers thick, and place your Cannabis shake into the center. Place a large ball-bearing or some clean metal washers in with the trim to weight the ball so it settles at the bottom of the water and stays there.**
2. **Twist the cloth, fold up the corners, to squeeze it into a ball, and tie shut. If needed refold back double so no material leaks from the bag. Fill your cooking pot three quarters full with water, and bring to a low boil.**
3. **Once the water is boiling, reduce heat to a slow boil, drop in the bag of plant shake, and let it sink before adding butter cubes. Slice butter into small pieces to help it melt faster.**
4. **Reduce heat to med-low and boil slowly for twenty minutes to a half hour, and remove from heat, leaving the bag submerged in the water and the butter floating on top. Let it cool to room temperature. Place the entire pot in the refrigerator to cool and for the butter to set. This makes the oil-infused butter harden, making it easy to collect.**

5. **When the entire mixture is cold, remove it from the refrigerator and crack the butter, and remove from the pot to be drained and dried for re-melting.**
6. **Melt the butter on low, and pour into a glass pan or baking dish, and place in the freezer to solidify.**
7. **To remove the squares from the glass dish, float them in hot water to warm the tray and release the butter cakes, and place upside down on the counter. Slice with a knife, and wrap each portion in paper or foil and freeze.**

Ingestion

Canna-butter has a rich, pleasant taste and is well suited to all kinds of treats, candies or beverages. Canna-butter can easily be used in all kinds of baked treats, known as 'medibles' which can deliver the Cannabinoids deep into the system in a sustained manner.

When Cannabis is ingested, it is metabolized through the liver first, and is then distributed by the blood through the entire system, activating receptors in the Endo-Cannabinoid system as it goes.

This makes ingestion the most effective use of Cannabis to relieve serious diseases like cancer or other diseases associated with the imbalance of the system.

Twisted Krispies

Ingredients:

- ¼ cup of Cannabis Butter,
- a teaspoon of vanilla
- half bag of Marshmallows
- four cups of rice crispy cereal
- dry resin if available

Melt the Cannabis butter, vanilla and marshmallows over low heat, stirring constantly, until marshmallows are melted. Add rice crisps and stir until cooled. Press into 8" x 8" pan and (optional) dust with dry resin.

Cool and cut into squares.

MAKING ICE-WATER HASH IN YOUR KITCHEN

Basic Tools

- Some water
- Two juice jugs
- 2 mixing bowls
- Medium Saucepan
- Nice fitting sieve
- Tea sieve
- Kitchen Whisk
- 90 micron silkscreen filter (art supply store)
- Drip coffee filter basket
- Paper filter
- 20 micron pressing filter
- Spray bottle
- A tray of ice cubes
- Paper towels
- Terrycloth hand towels

The method

Using the juice jug as a measure, fill the bowl about two-thirds full of cold water, and put the large sieve in. Place about an oz. of trim in the bowl, and use the whisk to gently press down and wet the material completely before placing in the half-crushed ice Let sit a few minutes to chill a bit, and begin gently mixing the shake.

The iced water will make trichomes stiffen up and tend to sink downward and through the sieve as you stir. The leaf materials need to be gently mixed and agitated for twenty minutes, turning it over in the filter to release resins and float them to the bottom.

Trichomes may also be carried down by carefully lifting and flooding the sieve to allow gravity to work in your favor. Occasionally lift the materials, and let the waters in the materials drain into the bowl to dislodge trichomes in the leaf. Allow to settle, and gently resubmerge before mixing some more.

Remove the sieve and material, and put aside in a bowl for a second rinse like the first. You can often get another 40 to 50% in additional Trichome weight by doing this. Pour the water from the bowl to your spare jug, to make filtering easier. Make certain to get all of the muddy-looking trichome sediments out of the bottom of the bowl, which is your hash.

Next, pour from the first jug through the 90 micron filter or a tea sieve into the second jug to remove the last of the plant particles and pistils, again making sure all the trichomes go through the filter into the second jug. Inspect the filter, and if needed, dip it and agitate it to release them into the water.

All of the water has to pass through the paper filter in order to catch and retain the liquid oils that are floating on the surface. Begin pouring the water through the paper filter into the final jug. This will take between 2 and 3 hours to finish, so patience is important. Oils that float on top of the water the entire time will not pass through the paper filter, and will eventually slow the water passing through to a crawl, but topping it up makes the larger part of the water pass through more quickly.

In the photo center left you can see the clear oil floating on top of the water, and up the edge of the paper filter. Trichomes and oils that gather on the side of the filter look like 'mud' while still wet with water. These oils and resins must be rinsed down the sides as it drains to be included with the blob of pure Trichomes at the bottom. This helps oils merge with the Trichomes as well.

A hand sprayer works well for this job, setting the nozzle to a jet so the solid stream will rinse the oil off the sides of the filter and allow it to collect and concentrate in the bottom with the hash. Keep the paper filter topped up during the process, the weight of a greater volume of water passes through faster, and shortens what can be a lengthy process.

All of the oils have been rinsed to the center of the filter, and the last bit of water is draining out. Once it has been properly drained, the resins collected may be placed filter and all in the deep freeze to solidify. This will allow it to be removed from the filter and make handling easier. Once the filter and hash are frozen, separate the hash from the filter, and place it on a flat and smooth oven-safe plate.

Preheat the oven to 170F and warm the hash-ball for 10 minutes, then remove and allow it to cool. Use a clean razor knife blade to remove the hash blob from the plate, and flip it over, and repeat the freeze and heating process until moisture stops coming out, and the hash has an oily feel.

Set the hash in the open so that the final moisture is allowed to evaporate, and blot gently, dabbing the ball with a paper towel to draw the water drops out. Squeezing it flat will also help the last of the water escape. The hash will also be quite oily and may flatten onto the plate. Once dry, it can be kept in a refrigerator to prevent the resins degrading, and help hold its shape as a solid.

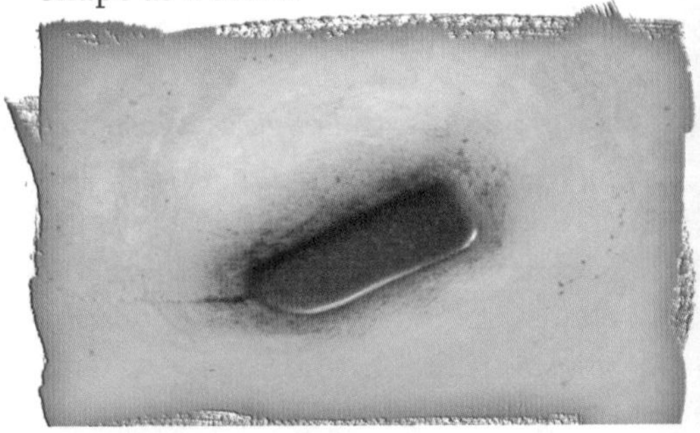

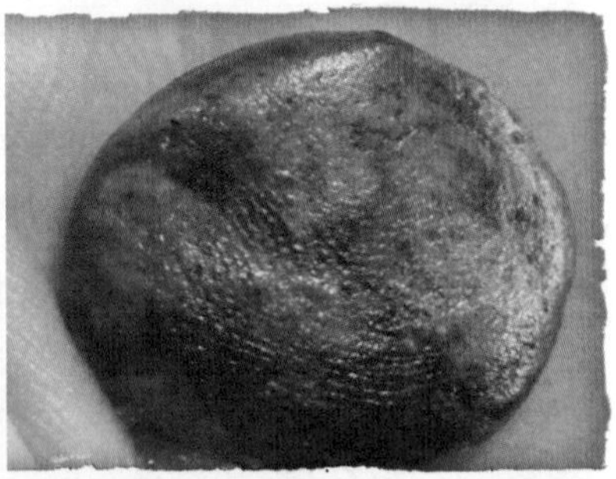

Materials

Materials may need to be treated carefully prior to processing into hash. If the trimmed material is too dry, it can be ground into a fine enough powder to pass through filters and end up contaminating the collected Trichomes. The best time to begin processing this material is when it is only partially dehydrated, and the pliable leaves will release oils and Trichomes without breaking up. The less fragmented the trim, the less filtering is required.

Dry materials may be rehydrated: place the trim in a container, spray with plain water, wetting well, cover and place in the refrigerator overnight prior to starting.

Medicinal Oils

Extracting the medicinal oils.

Four to eight ounces of leaf will make between twenty and thirty grams of potent oil. It's not necessary to make overly large quantities; it is easy to occasionally make smaller batches when you need them in your kitchen, using only an ounce or less at a time, soaking in a quart jar. Isopropyl alcohol or purest moonshine works best, and leaves the cleanest product and very little residues when finished. The best inner medicinal oil is made with a high CBD strain of Cannabis, and nothing is better to use than materials grown organically by you. Ask your seed vendor for information on which strain has the highest CBD content.

Take your dried leaf and grind to an even texture. Place the ground-up materials in a plastic bucket, pour isopropyl alcohol over the leaf until it is completely soaked and covered with solution.

Seal the container to keep dust out, and allow to sit at least a day to fully melt the Trichomes off the material and suspend it in the alcohol. Run the finished solution through a fine metal strainer to remove most of the leaf material, and then filter again through a paper filter so that any cellulose from the leaf will not go into the final solution.

Note: *The alcohol solution must be boiled below the evaporation temperature of the essential oils in the solution, about 180 degrees Fahrenheit. This will look like a low rolling boil.*

Removing the alcohol

Over-heating the solution will vaporize essential oils, and causes unwanted carbon compounds, potentially decreasing the potency and effectiveness of the medicines. Condensing the alcohol solution into medicinal oil can be extremely dangerous and requires a well-ventilated space because you will have to use some heat which will produce flammable fumes.

Patience is once again a good ally: evaporating at a lower temperature will take longer, but will be safer, and yield more of a higher quality product.

Fill the crock 3/4 full only, so the oils won't creep over the top of the rim and drip into the heater. When rings of oil form around the bowl, carefully roll the solution up over the rings to reintroduce it to the rest and keep it from burning on the crock. As the level drops from condensation, refill with additional solution and repeat, then boil down and cool the oil for cleaning.

The oils condense together and will form globs which are easily visible, and any other impurities that get separated in the process such as plant cellulose will show as patches of orange semi-clear between the oil patches.

A small slow-cooker with a three setting (Low Med and Hi) switch and porcelain inner crock pot works well.

The solution thickens as the alcohol evaporates.

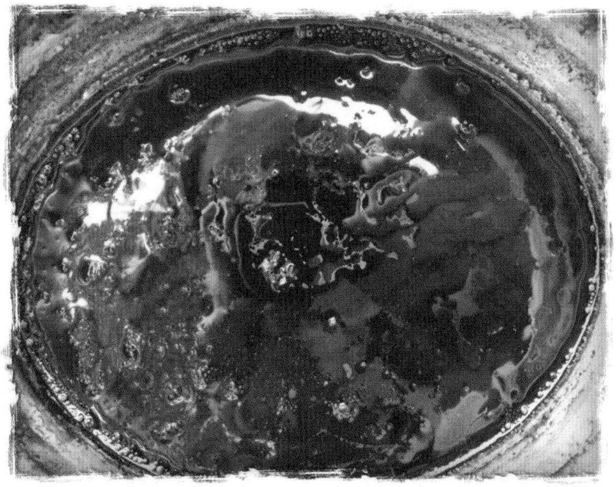

The red residue may be rinsed away with COLD water so resins aren't melted.

This material may easily be rinsed away using the following sequential method to clean the remaining sediments and plant materials out of your oil.

Cold water rinse

1. Condense your Cannabis-infused solution until the sharp smell of the alcohol has dissipated, and is replaced by an oily scent. Keep warming the oil until it has mostly finished bubbling.
2. Remove ceramic crock from the heater and allow cooling. The crock may be refrigerated or frozen to condense the oils and allow them to be collected.
3. Once the crock is cold, pour a little cold water in, and gently swirl around to collect and dissolve the residue seen in yellow pockets between the oil globules. Discard the dark-colored water and repeat until the water is fairly clear, and drain excess water.
4. Reheat the oil in the crock until all water droplets have evaporated, and the oil has returned to a glossy black color.
5. Repeat the step 3 rinsing process as often as it takes to clean the oil; usually two or three rinses will suffice. Once the oil is clean, the red and yellow pockets shown between the oil globules will be cleaned down to the bare bowl and the pure oil will have been left behind.
6. Re-warm the oil to get it to flow, and let it run into one end so you may collect it.
7. Syringes are a good choice for collecting and storing the medical oil, and make dispensing daily doses easy using gel caps for ingestion. Suck the oil into syringes while it is still warm.
8. Any residue left in the crock may be collected using a little alcohol and re-condense. Simply move the remaining oil solution to a metal measuring cup to finish. An electric coffee warmer is excellent for warming the small amount of oil until it bubbles off the remaining alcohol.
9. Pure Cannabis oil may be refrigerated or frozen for future use and to preserve the potency. Olive oil can be used as a carrying agent, but it has a shelf life of only a few weeks before it may become rancid.
10. Cannabis-infused oils should be used up as soon as possible, and can easily be substituted for Cannabutter although it is stronger and there is a definite green color and flavor.
11. The higher the quality of the starting material, the better the oil will be. The batch shown here was made using a few ounces of leaf, resulting in a dark green color from the chlorophyll in the leaves. Oils made from pure buds will be golden in color.

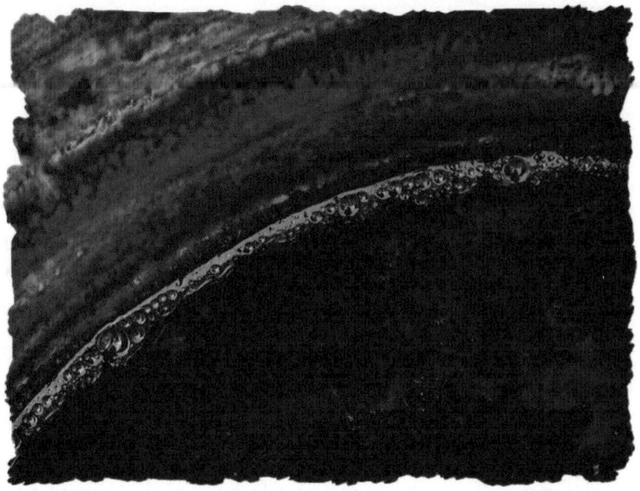

Bubbling at the edges as the last of the alcohol is being released.

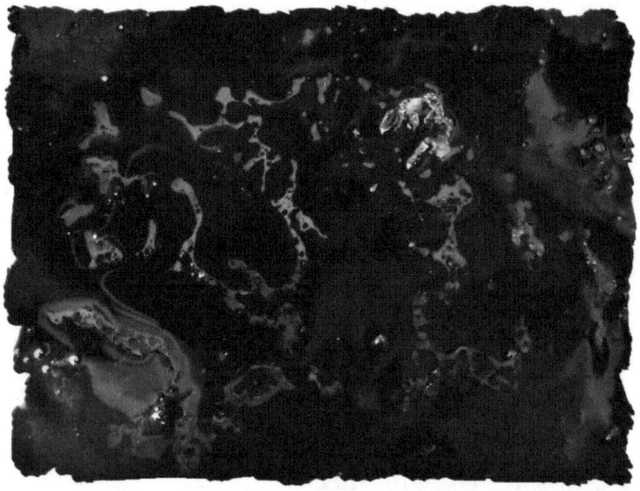

Oils are black blobs, the red translucent cellulose residue may be easily seen between the blobs.

After a cold water rinse, the residues are completely gone and the bowl shows white patches where they have been removed.

Dosing Medicinal Oils

In August of 2010, I was diagnosed with prostate cancer. I was told that radioactive therapy was my best choice, but there were possible side effects. Since I know that radioactivity is toxic to cells, I didn't receive this news well. My lay studies on Cannabis as medicine made the path I would follow clear, and I would never disobey my instinctive repulsion to unsafe treatments which may prematurely kill me. Having recommended it to others, I would rather take Cannabis as my own medicine too. Even more, I would never submit to treatments which I believe are experimental in nature, since there was no guarantee it would be successful.

The oncologist applied a lot of pressure to get me to submit to treatment, but finally I stood on my patient's right to refuse treatment by invoking the simple statement: "My body, my choice" and much to her chagrin opted for what is referred to as "watchful waiting." I would use Cannabis oil and rely on the very information I have been disseminating. Cannabis is Medicine and will cure cancer as shown by US studies in 1974.

I eventually convinced her to endorse my Health Canada application for Cannabis use by telling her that I require it for the stress of having been told I have cancer, and she reluctantly agreed. I immediately applied for a license from Health Canada to grow my medicine.

I must make honorable mention and express my appreciation to Rick Simpson, a Canadian activist and humanitarian who showed it was possible to cure cancer using even crudely made Cannabis oils for treatment, and has been subsequently sent into hiding in Europe. His story was an inspiration,and he is a hero who treated others for free. Rick's example helped me decide to treat myself with Cannabis oil and not rely on toxic radiation.

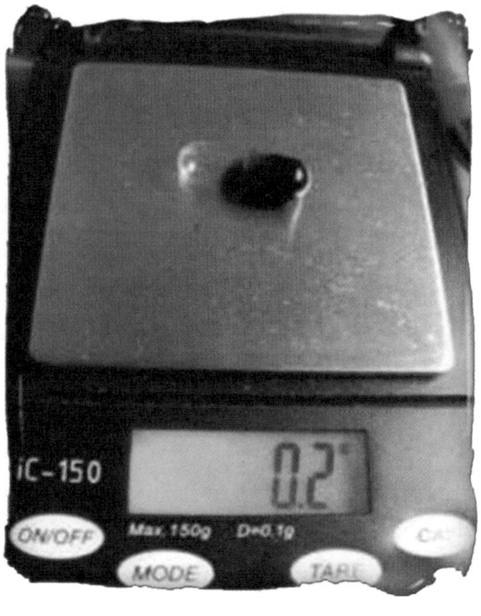

Here is how I manage and dispense my doses of Cannabis oil; the full dose is a gram of oil daily, dividing it into a number of smaller doses to be taken over the course of the day. While it was still warm, I sucked the oil up into a 10ml syringe sold for administering baby medicine.

I went to the local health food store and found some double-zero sized capsules; they are used by herbalists and health enthusiasts for supplements and other herbs. I use them to avoid having the odor on my breath, I don't mind the taste but not everyone else appreciates it.

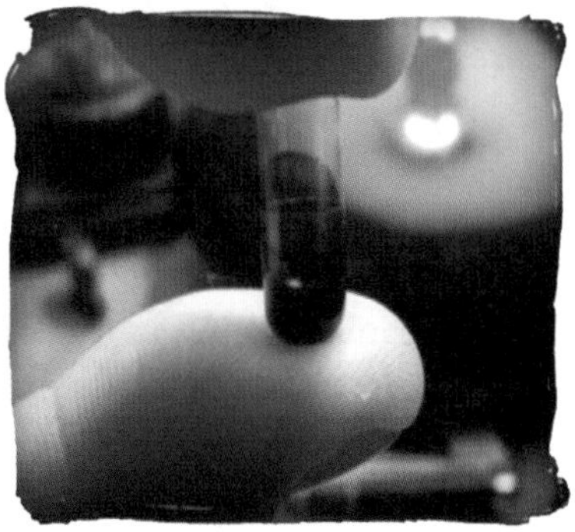

Cannabis oil is quite handy to dispense into capsules when it is contained in the syringe and refrigerated. Cooling it gives the oil a thick consistency like tar, which is great for storage, but makes it thick and can be hard to dispense. If you have your daily dose at room temperature you can easily squeeze it into the capsule before weighing it on an electronic scale.

Start with only a small amount, a single dose daily the size of a grain of rice, and double it every four days until you reach the full one-gram daily dosage. At that time you can divide the dosages as shown below, and take as many doses as add up to a full gram by weight.

It's a good idea to get a decent electronic scale that will weigh objects to a tenth of a gram. A good scale is essential for controlling dosage (very important). They are easy to pick up at your local electronics shop, and usually don't cost more than thirty dollars.

At full strength dosage, I take a capsule of .3 gm of oil 2 times, and the last dose for the end of the day I prepare at .4 grams to reach the full gram. The heavier last dose is helpful for sleep, and I always rest well. Rest is essential during treatment; it is natural that anxiety over having cancer can make rest difficult.

I am often asked if I am *stoned out of my mind* while dosing with the Cannabis oil, and the answer is: not beyond the first week. As you reach the higher doses it will make you sleepy for about the first week, but this effect wears off, and it is possible to function normally and do your day-to-day activities with little or no impairment. A common sense approach is best; Dosage can be made smaller in the morning so you can function, and heavier before bed, to induce rest.

Fact: *It is not possible to clinically overdose on Cannabis, since the LD50 rating is so low, at 1:40,000 it is one of the most non-toxic substances known to man.*

Cannabis Oil: First Time Dosing

First experiences dosing with Cannabis oil can be pretty intense for the first time user, so great care must be taken when inexperienced patients are dosing for the first time. The ingestion of Cannabis oils brings the full benefit of Cannabinoids to the body, easing the liver and resulting in homeostasis of the Endo-cannabinoid system.

The pain-relieving and relaxing effects from ingestion begin to take effect in as linle as a half hour, depending on the dose and body mass of the subject, but should be noticeable after an hour to two hours after taken. You will feel a slight "glow", you may feel slight pressure changes in your eyes, or you might break out in a linle sweat.

Laughter is normal. It is suggested you should make sure the seing in which you take it is familiar and comfortable, with encouraging and supportive friends and family around you.

Some common effects are: pain relief , tension relief, heightened sense of awareness and creativity, but may include feeling 'high' dizziness, giggling, hunger and sleepiness.

If you feel 'high', try to remember that Cannabis oil is a non-toxic sub-stance, and can't harm you in any way. Cannabinoids do not affect the autonomic reflex system the way pain relieving opioids do. You can over-dose, on Cannabis oil, and simply sleep the effects off with no harm other than a slight hangover at most. Your body may not be accustomed to Cannabinoids, however once you adjust your dose to the correct amount for your needs, this won't bother you, and you may occasionally enjoy the relaxing effects.

If you get dizzy recline to a couch where you may relax or stretch out.

If you are a patient who has a painful condition, you may not feel some of the aforementioned effects, and only notice an overall abatement of pain. This is especially true for chronic arthritis sufferers.

When using concentrated cannabis oil it is recommended that you stay hydrated with water. Even if you're not doing anything, your body's metabolism is raised using cannabis oil. Always keep water around you.

Pay anention to how your body feels. If you feel anxious, in most cases a simple snack or some water should help you feel bener. It's best to dose on a full stomach to avoid these types of complications.

Quality is an important factor, careful consideration should be taken when choosing. Oil that isn't made from the entire plant may lack key components. The amount of THC in the oil is determined by the ratios of flowering material and trim used to make the oil. Other factors include the strength of a particular strain.

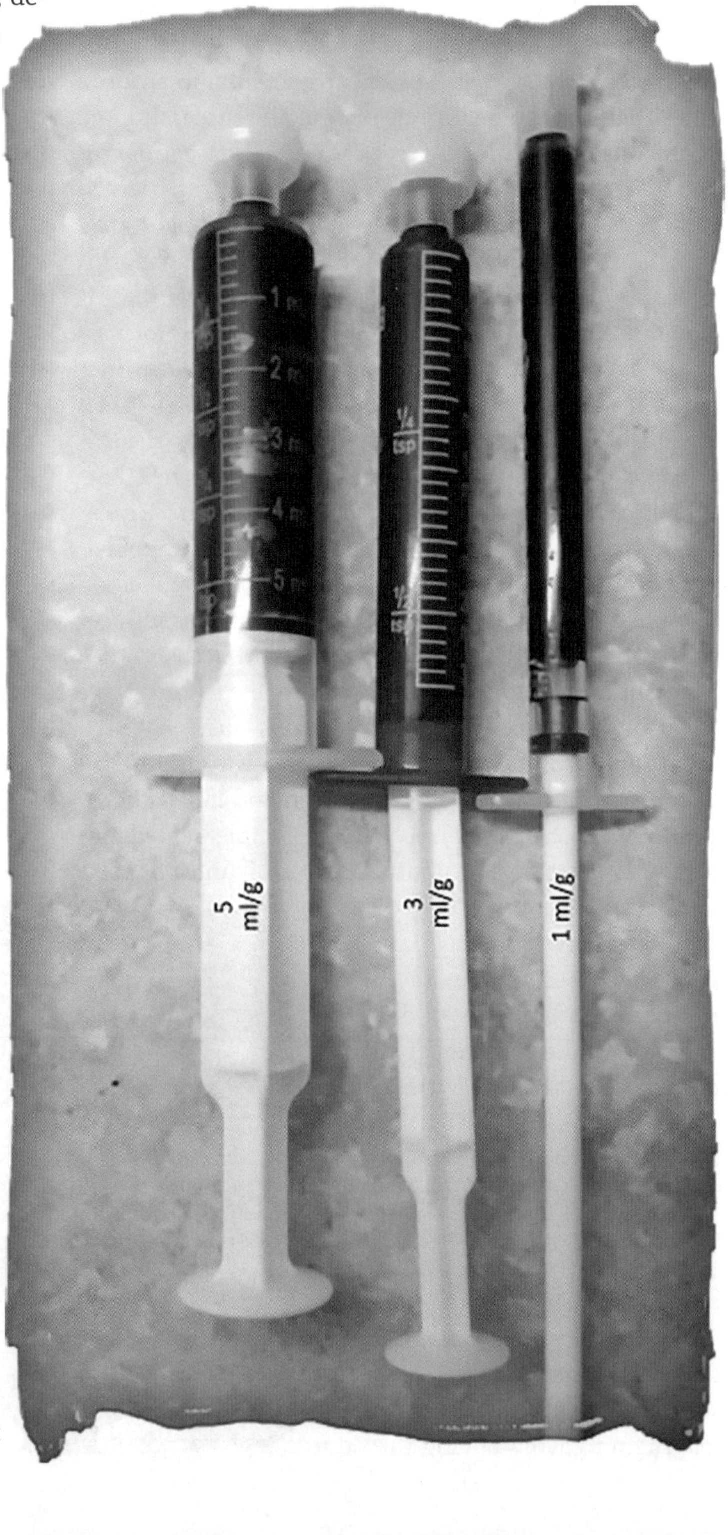

Cannabis Oil: Understanding Quantities

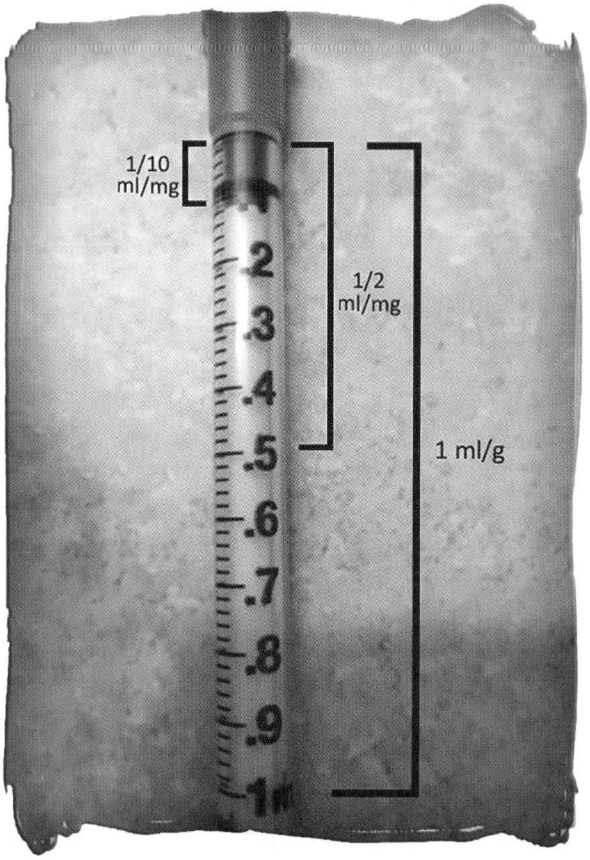

Dosages for Cannabis oil are measured in milligrams, but they are packaged in syringes of various sizes. 1 ml is equal to one gram of medicine. Pictured left is a one gram (1 ml/1 gram) syringe, which I am showing empty for the purpose of observing the measurement for doses. As you can see the syringe is divided in ten. Each part is .1 ml/gm.

A syringe of the one gm/ml size might last ten days for some-one using .1 ml/gm per day for light pain, five days at .2 ml/gm, and so on.

The recommended dose for the first time is .50 ml/gm, or one half of one tenth of a gram, a very small amount, about the size of one half the a grain of rice.

The three gm/3000ml syringe is pictured lower left. The syringe is divided in three with ten parts per gram. Each part is .010 ml/gm. This is used for normally dosing patients.

The 5gm/5000ml syringe is used when large quantities are needed for curing, as in the case of cancer, withdrawal from opiates and alcohol.

Large syringes such as the 10 gm/1000ml are also commonly used when a patient is dosing for the sake of cure, as larger quantities need to be used when the body is in crisis.

Finally, the bottom photograph shows all three syringes in the filled state, and ready to use.

As you can see, the color of the oil can make it difficult to read the markings on the syringe, especially the 1gm size.

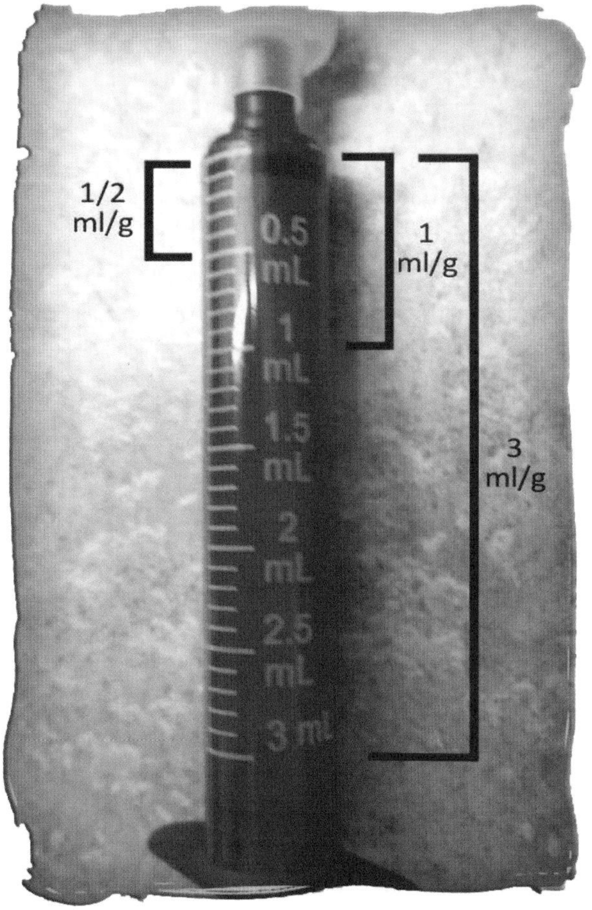

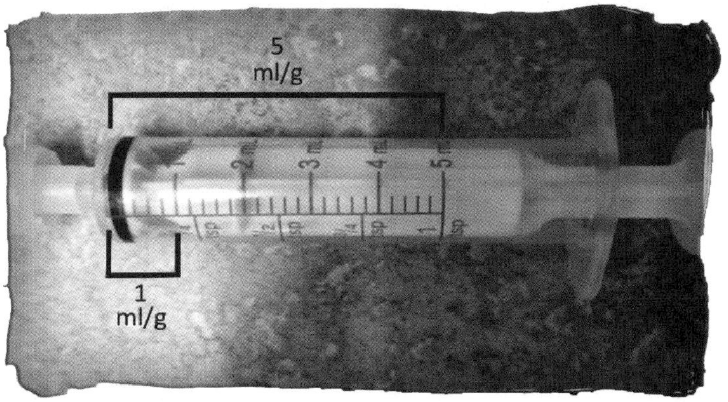

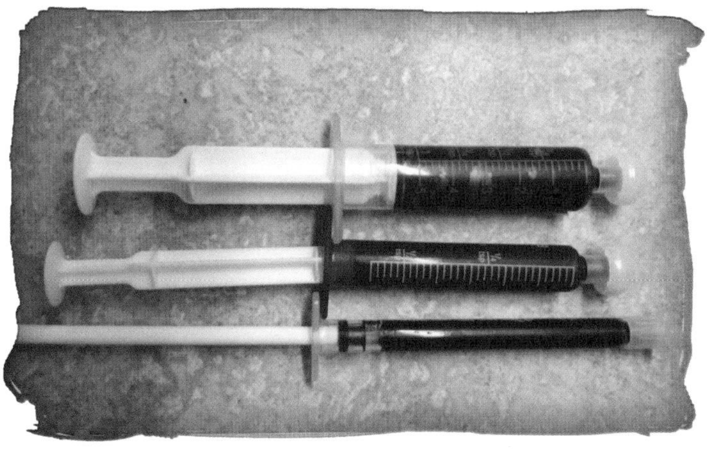

Dosing can be done using fillable plant based capsules, and several sizes are manufactured and produced. They are made in vegetarian base, bovine base (if you aren't concerned) with multiple flavors and in a full spectrum of colors.

In the table to the right, the sizes of the pill **sizes** have been correlated to the **dose range**. These capsules may be bought online, and used to regulate doses by color code for easy dose recognition.

Each application of Cannabis oil for the relief of discomfort, pain, or disease has its own dosage, more or less depending on the severity of the disease. Dose downward for recommended doses given to find your personal dosage level. Dosages may also be specific as to type (Indica for pain and sleep, Sativa for depression and anxiety) so it is important to know which types will benefit you in the most efficient way at different times of the day.

Cap Size		Approx. Volume
5	=	78 mg. to 156 mg.
4	=	120 mg. to 240 mg.
3	=	150 mg. to 300 mg.
2	=	200 mg. to 400 mg.
1	=	300 mg. to 600 mg.
0	=	400 mg. to 800 mg.
0E	=	462 mg. to 924 mg.
00	=	600 mg. to 1100 mg.
000	=	800 mg. to 1600 mg.

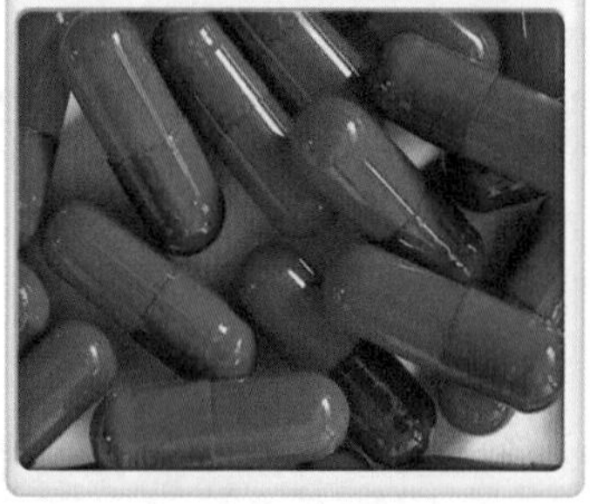

Introductory dosing needs to be gradual to acclimatize the body. During week one, the correct dose is the size of a half a grain of rice.

Week One	.05 gm/ml daily	Size:
Week Two	.10 gm/ml daily	Size
Week Three	.25 gm /ml daily	Size:
Week Four	.50 gm/ml daily	Size:

WEEK FIVE ON.	Full dosage	Titrate as needed
Cancer		
Morning dose:	**Afternoon Dose**	**Evening dose:**
.25 gm	.25 gm	.50 gm
Arthritis		
Morning dose:	**Afternoon Dose**	**Evening dose:**
.10 gm	.10 gm	.25 gm
Withdrawal:	Selective Seratonin uptake inhibitors.	
.20 gm	.20 gm	.20

Notes

Dosing methods

Dosing with Cannabis is a remedy which is thousands of years old, and can be used for a very many curative purposes Dosing with oil means ingesting, placing in body cavities and topical applications rather than smoking.

Whether one uses a capsule, with food, or just squeezing it onto your finger and orally ingesting it, the point is to get it into your body in a concentrated form and receive the full medicinal benefits. Obviously, smoking is not as efficient delivery as ingesting.

Some of the common human ailments which the Chinese texts say are helped medicinally by Cannabis include: chronic arthritis, alcoholism and drug addiction etc. and modern studies have confirmed the Chinese wisdom as fact. Recently, studies show results in curing viral infections, like HIV and Hepatitis C, mental disorders, skin lesions, cancerous growths in all parts of the body.

Preparations for stepping down the potency of Cannabis oil

There are instances when the potency of oils must be diluted or stepped down. One of the best methods of this is infusion in fat soluble oil, such as grape seed oil, olive oil, or coconut oil. Generally, methods may vary, from putting the dried and prepared plant matter into the oil and simmering it to combining prepared oil concentrates with its relevant companion oil.

Some of the reasoning behind this dilution may include: introductory dosing for patients who are new to dosing with Cannabis, conscientiously dosing patients relative to body mass, as in the case of juveniles or pets, light dosing for arthritic pain, maintenance dosing for patients recovering after cancer treatments, relief of nausea and many other applications where full strength Cannabis oil is not needed or the patient cannot inhale or vaporize. In terms of ingestion, infused oil may be more quickly absorbed into the system, allowing the medicine to reach the site of disease more quickly.

Coconut oil has the added advantage of being approximately equal in weight and volume to Cannabis oil extracts which, while being an excellent infusion medium for Cannabis oils, also makes it much easier to measure accurately and combine the two to achieve a reasonably accurately derived percentage-based solution.

As indicated in the bar graph. Each different dilution can have a separate use.

1. 50%
2. 33%
3. 25%
4. 20%
5. 16%
6. 11%
7. 10%
8. 5%

1:1 50%	1:2 33%	1:4 25%	1:5 20%	1:6 16%	1:9 11%	1:10 10%

Diluting oils for potency regulation allows the patient to more precisely dose below the level of intoxication, relieving pain with the very minimum of side effects. Unlike other medicines, patients are required to titrate down from a standard dose to achieve workable potency while avoiding unwanted side effects.

Noah's Tale of Treating ADHD with Cannabis Oils

I am Noah. I am 17, just finishing grade eleven and at a critical point in my life. I know I need to decide what kind of career path I'm going to take, but because of my ADHD it can be hard to focus and relax during stressful times in class, whether it is a simple quiz, or my final exam.

Medicinally, the Sativa side of RSO helps keep my ADHD down, by keeping me focused and on task. The Indica-dominant part keeps my Tourette syndrome under control and relaxes my body enough so I can easily control my tics. I also managed to find out that if you dab a very small amount, it hits you with pure Indica effects and is really good for right before you go to bed.

Cannabis oil has helped me greatly in these times of stress. Its effects last between four to six hours (depending on the dosage) and the potency of the high-quality oil helps me stay relaxed, so I can do my work in a more peaceful state of mind.

The method I use to take the oil is this: I place the dosage (approximately 0.1 g) on a chewable vitamin. The vitamin I use and find works the most is XXXXXXX (GABA), a neurotransmitter that creates a fast-acting, calming effect that helps add to my relaxation. The GABA doesn't have sedative effects, but instead, relaxes your mind and muscles and gives you more control over stress. I place the vitamin with RSO-side stuck to the inside of my cheek and leave it in there for 10 minutes and then chew and swallow whatever is left over.

Before I started using RSO and Cannabis in general, I was on countless different ADHD drugs and managed to titrate off them until I was only on one. The last pharmaceutical I was on was Biphentin and when I started using RSO, I was able to eventually come off of that pharmaceutical, as well.

Because the strain that has been predominantly used in the Cannabis oil I've had access to is RockStar which is an Indica dominant hybrid, it's mostly a body-high that relaxes me more physically than mentally, but it still has the lingering, sativa head-high I need to focus during the long lectures my English teacher loves to give.

Although there's a pretty fine line between barely feeling the RSO's effects and it being a little too much to handle, after testing different dosages for about a week at home, I easily found the right dosage I need to be both completely functional, while still experiencing the RSO's needed medicinal effects.

Noah Kirkman

Building a Green-Hut

Here's my original design for a PVC summer hut, made from one-inch light piping, corrugated plastic sheets, and five basic molded PVC parts. The hut features a 45 degree roof with a 6½ foot peak and all Coroplastic reflective white walls and semi-clear roof sheets, but can easily be covered with UV 0.5 ml plastic sheeting: Designed to be very bright on the inside and provide enough room to cultivate.

Its simply assembled from five molded parts and pipe lengths, and ten sheets of coroplastic and can easily be expanded in size to suit your needs. This one is built in four sections with a finished dimension of 8x10 feet.

Including the Coroplastic sheets, the cost of building it was around three hundred-fifty dollars. Some of the molded parts had to be obtained online, but most of the equipment and supplies needed to finish this durable shed were available from local sources in the plastics and signage industry.

It is indeed ironic to me that all the plastic parts for this hut are presently made from petroleum products. This serves only to illustrate yet another example of the control of big oil. All of the extruded and molded products could be made of plastics created from hemp cellulose.

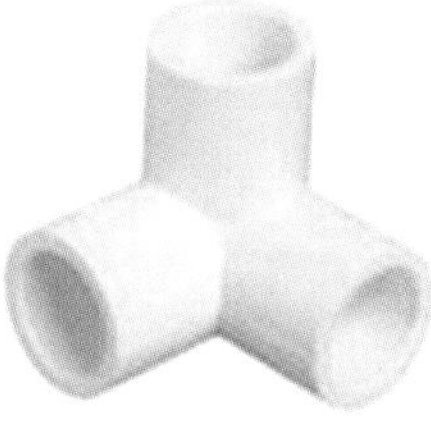

3-way fittings

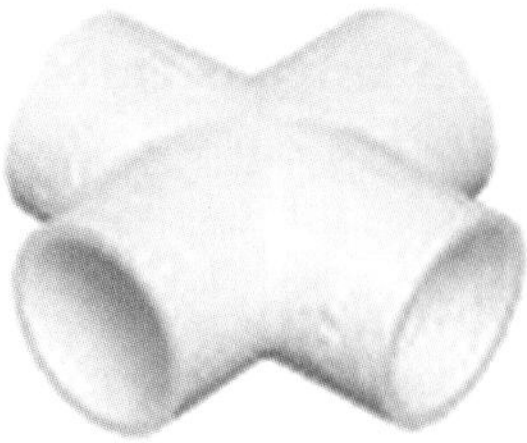

T-fittings

When you order, remember to specify 10-footers so there will be less waste. I got the guy to buck these 20-footers in half.

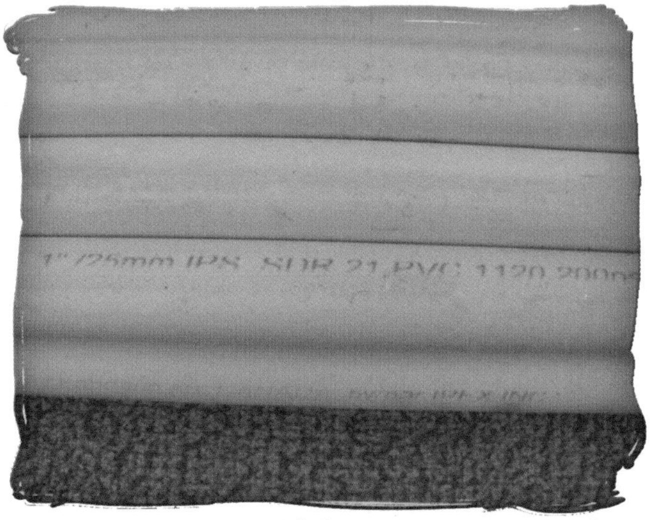

This shows the type. Thin walled 125mm 200 PSI pipe used for lawn sprinklers.

T– sliders

22 degree Y-fittings

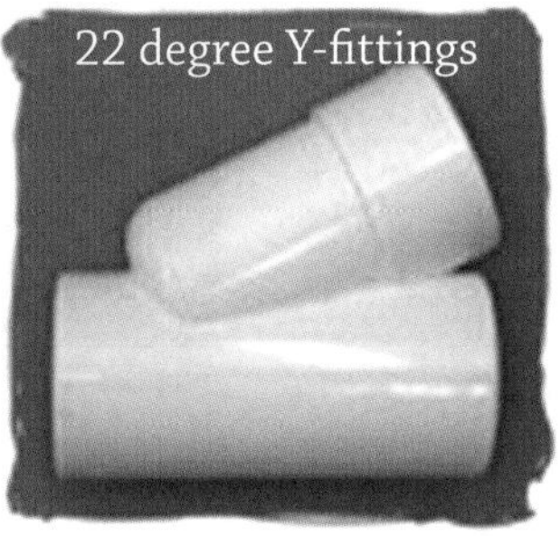

22 degree elbows

Tools Needed

Finishing saw or miter saw and box
Tape measure
A steel file for deburring the pipe ends
Industrial Razor safety knife

Covering

Coroplastic or clear Green-house sheets, 4x8 - 10 sheets
Or 240 sq feet of 2.5 to 5 ml plastic roll

Molded PVC Parts List

300 ft 125mm SDR21 pipe
PVC Cement
PVC Plumbers tape
3-way fittings (corners) 8 pieces
Cross fittings (center gables) 3 pieces
T-fittings (walls and end gables) 20 pieces
22 degree Y-fittings (Gable ends) 10 pieces
22 degree elbows (Gable peak) 10 pieces
T– sliders 4 pieces

Miscellaneous Parts

6 to 8 inch Zip-Ties, 200 pieces
Transparent duct tape

Walls

'W1' Uprights: 4 foot 10 inch length, 16 pieces
'W2' Lateral sections: 28 inch length, 20 pieces
'W3' End Wall sections: 92 inch length, 4 pieces

Gables

'G1' Rafter pieces: 47 inch length, 10 pieces
'G2' Lower brace: 92 inch length, 5 pieces
'S1' Spacers: 2 inch length, 10 pieces

Pre-cut all your pipe parts to the correct lengths using a miter saw to ensure a clean and square cut. File to debur the ends to a slight bevel. When they are glued this will ensure strong joints.

Before you start to assemble the hut, I recommend you be sure to press-fit together the walls without any adhesive, these materials are light enough to preassemble a section easily and check the measurements of parts.

Performing test fits of all the components of this project should be a default procedure, before cementing sections together and will help ensure the success of the project.

Place a pair of temporarily assembled gables on top of the press-fitted walls, checking where the overhang ends just to see how the measurements are working out. The 'Y' fitting on the ends of the gables should sit squarely on the top of the wall, and make an overhang of a few inches, and the end gables should line up exactly to sit on top of the end wall.

Assemble the walls without the 3-ways on them as shown, and attach them to the completed end sections.

The first gables are assembled, attached at the top and bottom to form the first section of the roof.

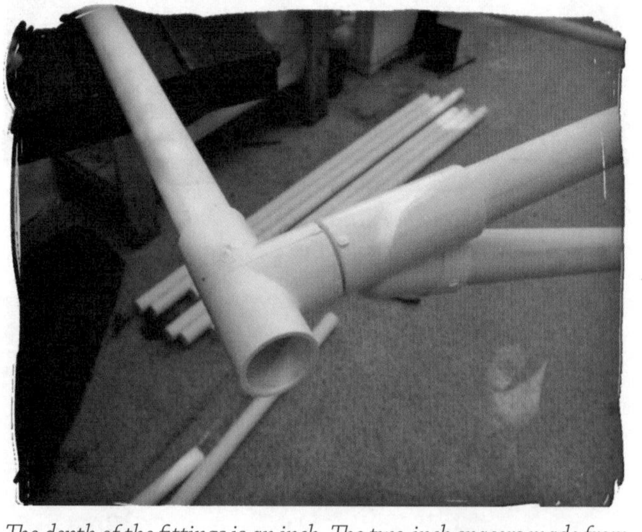

The depth of the fittings is an inch. The two-inch spacers made from pipe help attach the gable to the overhang section.

Wall Assembly

Assemble the wall section on a flat surface using eight of the W2 parts per side, from the center out, by connecting two W1's and complete the walls final end piece with the three way on the ends as shown left. Cement together and let set.

Start with six 'W1' four-foot ten-inch uprights. Make sure the T fitting is perfectly aligned to the one on the opposite end, then cement the tee fittings and allow them to set.

Connect eight lateral W2 sections to the T fittings on the first three uprights and finish the ends with the 3-way connectors, and complete the wall section with a 4'10" plain pipe. Repeat this to make the other wall, and let the cement set once again. Make four additional W1 uprights with tee snap fittings for the center wall supports, and fit them onto the W3 92" end-wall lengths, then pre-fit the end wall sections to the walls, and test for square and width. Install the end walls without cement for portability of the unit.

End wall construction isn't the same as the side walls, the upright supports use a snap T fitting instead, so the wall may be disassembled for moving or flat storage. Slide the fittings over the pipe and position before fitting the ends into the finished side wall sections.

Above, the frame is being test fitted. The ten-foot walls have been fully assembled to the corners first, and the eight-foot lengths are added to the end.

Install end walls with snap-tee uprights, and begin building the gables, starting with an assembled pair and attaching sections to each other with W2 sections between teed ends and gable peaks.

Temporarily tie down gable ends at the corners to the top bar of the walls using 6" zip ties, and complete once the entire gable assembly is constructed, checking for overlap and square.

Once the entire frame has been constructed, it can be covered with greenhouse plastic, or fitted coroplastic panels using zip-ties to attach to the frame.

The door can easily be fitted with coroplastic as well, and joints at the corners of the building may be covered with clear duct tape to seal the cracks.

An additional feature of the white coroplastic walls is the retention and reflection of light within the hut. A semi-clear plastic roof works well enough, but clear greenhouse grade UV coroplastic panels would be the most effective to allow maximum light in the top.

One-foot panels go on the walls first, then a four-foot sheet on top to fill the wall panel.

End gable joints need to be solid to bear the weight of the top. Use the gable as a template to cut your end gable panels before you assemble them

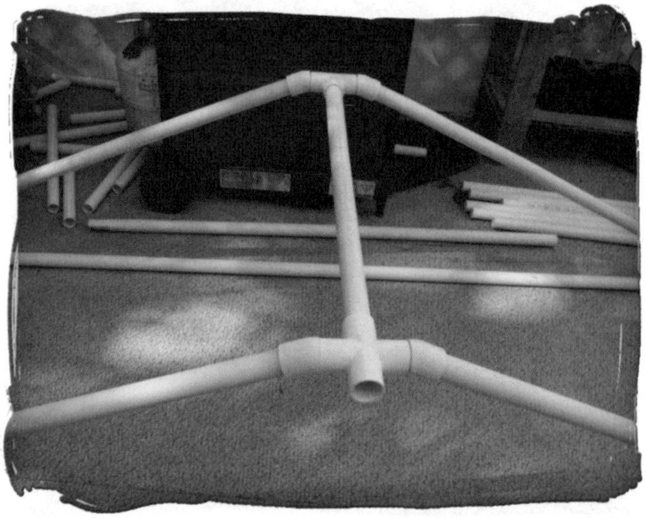

End gables use a T fitting, while the center gables are assembled using a cross fitting at the peak

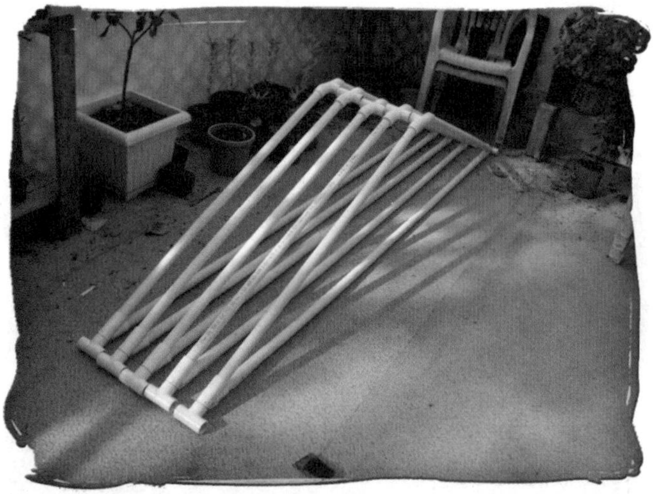

You don't need to use any cement at the top of the gable, gravity will hold the joint in place. This allows the joint to be turned as its assembled, and helps prevent crooked joints.

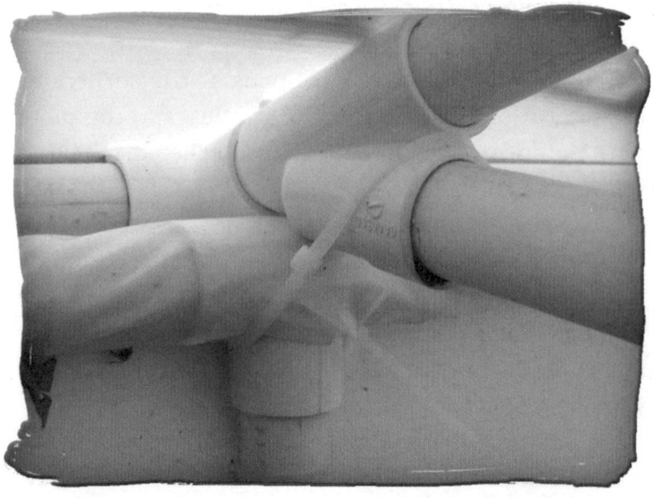

The end joints need to be strong as they hold the weight of the gable frame and covering once the roof is finished.

Hut positioning is important too. Here, rain tends to fall down behind the hut, soaking the floor during every rain storm. A 90° rotation corrected this and made it dry again.

The hut can be anchored to a deck, or positioned in the corner of a deck to prevent it being blown away by a heavy wind.

Here, I have also used concrete bricks to assist in stabilizing the position of the hut.

3.5 mil plastic can be used for the roof, and attached with duct tape, but it only lasts about a year due to sun damage sustained during the summer months.

Once the hut was constructed, I realized the gable cross-braces were a bit of a hazard while moving around the hut. I replaced them with a central post to keep the roof in shape.

Lightweight, adjustable shelving around the walls work well for raising up smaller plants closer to the brighter light at the top of the hut.

It's easy to strap a power bar to any pipe to power the hut's timers, lights, fans, bubblers and sound system.

You may or may not need lights in your hut, but you will need air circulation inside to keep all your plants breathing properly.

The solid construction of the gables means oscillating fans can easily be hung from the gable cross bars near one end of the building to provide adequate air circulation and allow every plant to be slightly shaken by cross breezes.

Once the hut has had all its edges sealed, it will allow any plants to survive well into the autumn season, keeping frost off the plants and especially allowing northern strains of Cannabis to finish up completely.

I hope you build it and add your own touches.

HARVEST QUALITY REPORT

Here's a report you can copy and print or simply use as a guide when harvesting your crop.

PHYSICAL EXAMINATION

1. ______ Visual Appeal
Rate the visual appeal of the buds from 1-10 unappealing-excellent.

2. ______Visible Trichomes
Rate the visible trichome content from 1-10 none-totally covered.

3. Use an X to indicate the colors that are present in the trichome heads under magnification or list the percentages of each color for a more precise report. Leave these fields blank if you do not have a powerful magnifier.

Clear ____
Cloudy ____
Amber ____
Dark ____

4. Mark with X the colors that are present in the buds or for a more detailed color analysis rate presence on a scale 1-9 light-dark.

Brown ____
Green ____
Gold ____
Blue ___
Grey ____
White ____
Red ____
Rust ____
Orange ____
Purple ____
Black ____

5. ____ Bud density
Rate the bud density from 1-10 airy-dense. For samples that are not in their natural state leave this field blank.

6. Use numbers 1-9 on descriptors that apply to the aroma of freshly broken bud where a one indicates a subtle presence and 9 indicates a pronounced presence. Delete the existing space when marking a descriptor in order to maintain the columns in alignment.

Ammonia __	Earthy __	Licorice __	Peach __
Berry __	Floral __	Mango __	Pepper __
Blueberry __	Fruit __	Meat __	Petroleum __
Bubblegum __	Grape __	Melon __	Pine __
Cedar __	Grapefruit__	Menthol __	Pineapple __
Cherry __	Grass/Hay __	Mint __	Rotten __
Chocolate __	Hash __	Mold __	Skunk __
Citrus __	Iron/Rust __	Musk __	Spice __
Coconut __	Leather __	Nutmeg __	Strawberry__
Coffee __	Lemon __	Orange __	Vanilla __

7. ____ Aroma
Rate the aroma from 1-10 repulsive-delightful. Use freshly crumbled bud for best results.

8. ____ Seed content
Rate seed content from 0-10 none-fully seeded.

9. ____ Weeks cured
If known enter the number of weeks your sample has been cured. If desired repeat SSR after an additional two weeks of curing.

PHYSICAL EXAMINATION COMMENTS:

____
____
____

THE SMOKE TEST

1. Please use a clean instrument for the evaluation. Enter information below that will identify the instrument as follows: Address these questions while smoking.

Water pipe (bong, hookah, bubbler etc)____________
Vaporizer (brand name) ____________________
Pipe (size-type, i.e. medium-glass) ______________
Joint (brand of papers) ____________________
Other (specify) ________________________

2. Use numbers 1-9 on descriptors that apply to the taste. A one indicates a subtle presence and a nine indicates a very pronounced presence. Delete the existing space when marking a descriptor in order to maintain the columns in alignment.

Ammonia __Earthy __ Licorice __ Peach __
Berry __ Floral __ Mango __ Pepper __
Blueberry __ Fruit __ Meat __ Petroleum __
Bubblegum __ Grape __ Melon __ Pine __
Cedar __ Grapefruit__ Menthol __ Pineapple __
Cherry __ Grass/Hay __ Mint __ Rotten __
Chocolate __ Hash __ Mold __ Skunk __

Citrus __Iron/Rust __ Musk __ Spice __
Coconut __ Leather __ Nutmeg __ Strawberry__
Coffee __ Lemon __ Orange __ Vanilla __

If appropriate return to this question after 5-10 minutes and mark with X any unmarked descriptors for lingering aftertaste.

3. ____ Taste
Rate your impression of the taste from 1-10 unpleasant-delicious.

4. ____ State of dryness
Rate the dryness of the bud from 1-10 wet-dry where 5 is ideal.

5. ____ Smoke-ability
Rate the smoke ability of the sample from 1-10 harsh-smooth.

6. ____ Smoke expansion
Rate how the smoke expands in the lungs from 1-10 stable-explodes.

SMOKE TEST COMMENTS:

____
____
____

FOLLOW-UP QUESTIONS

Address final questions immediately after effects have worn off.

1. ____ Dosage
Enter the number of hits taken to reach desired effects.

2. ____ Effect onset
Rate how quickly the effect hit from 1-10 immediate-major creeper.

3. ____ Sativa influence
Rate the sativa influence detected from 0-10 none-extreme. Sativa influence is best described as a clear and energetic mental effect.

4. ____ Indica influence
Rate the Indica influence detected from 0-10 none-extreme. Indica influence is best described as a sedative, lethargic or numbing effect on the body.

5. ____ Potency
Rate the potency of the sample from 0-10 none-devastating.

6. ____ Duration
Indicate the number of hours the effects lasted.

7. ____ Tolerance build up
Rate how quickly tolerance builds from 0-10 none-rapid. Leave this field blank if you have not used this sample repeatedly.

8. Usability
Rate on a scale of 1-9. A one indicates the worst time of day to consume this strain and a nine represents the ideal time of day. Leave fields blank if you have not yet formed an opinion.

Morning: wake up __ Day: work __ Evening: relax __ Night: sleep __

9. ____ Overall satisfaction
Rate your overall satisfaction from 1-10 poor-Holy Grail.

10. ____ Ability and conditions
Rate your overall ability to judge from 1-10 low-high. Consider experience, strain familiarity, atmosphere, current tolerance and most importantly the condition and preparation of the sample.

11. Judging from the sample alone do you personally consider this strain a keeper for long term use?

Yes __ No __

12. Rate the noticeable effects on a scale of 1-9 mild-severe. Take care to use the appropriate column for your response. Delete the existing space when recording your entry to maintain the columns in alignment. In all cases these casual observations should not be construed as medical advice.

Negative/Positive Effect

____|____ Appetite
____|____ Anxiety relief
____|____ Paranoia relief
____|____ Sex drive
____|____ Sleep
____|____ Pain relief
____|____ Ability to rest or sit still
____|____ Thought process
____|____ Speech process
____|____ Imagination/creativity
____|____ Humor perception
____|____ Visual perception
____|____ Audio perception
____|____ Taste perception

EXTENDED MEDICAL SURVEY (optional)
Describe any benefits you receive from the use of this strain, and report and adverse effects.

Negative/ Positive Effect

__[ ]__ __[ ]__ Alcoholism/Alcohol Abuse
__[ ]__ __[ ]__ Allergic rhinitis
__[ ]__ __[ ]__ Amphetamine Dependence
__[ ]__ __[ ]__ Anorexia
__[ ]__ __[ ]__ Arthritis/Musculoskeletal pain
__[ ]__ __[ ]__ Asthma/Cough
__[ ]__ __[ ]__ Bipolar disorder
__[ ]__ __[ ]__ Cancer/Cancer Chemotherapy
__[ ]__ __[ ]__ Chronic fatigue
__[ ]__ __[ ]__ Depression
__[ ]__ __[ ]__ Diarrhea
__[ ]__ __[ ]__ Epilepsy
__[ ]__ __[ ]__ Glaucoma
__[ ]__ __[ ]__ Hiccough
__[ ]__ __[ ]__ High blood pressure/Racing pulse
__[ ]__ __[ ]__ Insomnia
__[ ]__ __[ ]__ Itching
__[ ]__ __[ ]__ Migraine/vascular headache
__[ ]__ __[ ]__ Muscle Spasm
__[ ]__ __[ ]__ Muscular movement disorders
__[ ]__ __[ ]__ Nausea
__[ ]__ __[ ]__ Panic Attacks
__[ ]__ __[ ]__ Peripheral nerve pain
__[ ]__ __[ ]__ Post traumatic Stress Disorder
__[ ]__ __[ ]__ Pre-Menstrual Syndrome
__[ ]__ __[ ]__ Sedative/Opiate Dependence
__[ ]__ __[ ]__ Schizophrenia
__[ ]__ __[ ]__ SLE - systemic lupus erythematosus
__[ ]__ __[ ]__ Spasticity in Multiple Sclerosis

FINAL COMMENTS AND OBSERVATIONS:

Growing Guide

Use the spaces below to keep notes on your plants.

Week One: Germinate

Day/Tips

Tip of the Week

Keep lights close to the seedlings to prevent stretching. Strong circulating and oscillating fan helps build strong stems.

Day 1

Start your beans with the method on the previous page. They may take 5-7 days to germinate.

Day 2.

Check daily for sprouts, they may even emerge as soon as the second day. Plant as soon as they pop!

Day 3.

Open the bag daily to refresh air, it prevents mold which can kill the tender seeds.

Day 4.

Seedlings get water but no fertilizer for 2 weeks.

Day 5.

Don't let the seeds over-heat or get too cold. A consistent 75F is ideal for germination.

Day 6.

A small beverage cup with holes poked in the bottom works great for seed planting.

Day 7.

Plant sprouted beans 1/4 inch deep in soil as soon as the root pops out the pointed end.

C4/LP
F2B
C4/LP
OGK
BSW
B.Blast
AZ Gold
OGK
BBlast
AZ Gold
OGK
BBlast
AZ Gold

Week Two: Plant your beans!

Day/Task

Tip of the Week

Take note of how fast your pots dry out, be careful not to over-water. Moist, but not wet.

Day 8

Keep a fan blowing on the seedlings to strengthen the stems.

Day 9

Day 10

Day 11

Day 12

Day 13

Day 14

Week Three:

Day/Task

Tip of the Week

Don't set your lights too high, or the seedlings will stretch for the light. CFL lights can be as close as two inches to the tops without burning them.

Day 15

Its time to flush your pots to clear and fertilize.

Day 16

Use your 9-11-11 tomato food to encourage vegetative growth.

Day 17

Day 18

Day 19

Day 20

Day 21

Week Four:

Day/Task

Tip of the Week

Time to pot up to the next size, check the pots for root-bound, add an inch to two inches to the pot size each time.

Day 22

Rooted clones can be ready to bloom in four weeks! Pot up and use your 9-11-11 tomato food to encourage vegetative growth.

Day 23

Day 24

Day 25

Day 26

Day 27

Day 28

Week Five:

Day/Task

Tip of the Week

Seedlings may be forced into flower starting in about the fifth week. A dark period will help trigger them. Clones may be forced anytime, because they are already mature.

Day 29

While the plants are small, keep the space small too, and the lights bright to maximize effect.

Day 30

Day 31

Day 32

Day 33

Day 34.

Day 35

Week Six:

Day/Task

Tip of the Week

Cuttings can be taken from the inner branches for sexing.

Day 36

Couldn't hurt to pot up since they should be root-bound again.

Day 37

Day 38

Day 39

Day 40

Day 41

Day 42

Week Seven:

Day/Task

Tip of the Week

Cannabis loves Magnesium, which can be applied using a molasses flush: One teaspoon of Molasses dissolved in a gallon of water.

Day 43

Day 44

Day 45

Day 46

Day 47

Day 48.

Day 49

Week Eight:

Day/Task

Tip of the Week

Normally all Cannabis plants will be ready to flower once 2 months old. Patience will get you a better harvest, simply extend the veg time before flowering.

Day 50

Potting time again? Well at least check and see how the roots are looking. Your call.

Day 51

Day 52

Day 53

Day 54

Keep a close eye out for early maturing males! Little clusters form near the base of branches.

Day 55

Day 56

Week Nine:

Day/Task

Tip of the Week

If you're using mature clones, flower from here to the end of the schedule.

Day 57

Day 58

Day 59

Day 60

Eight weeks is the normal time for a Cannabis plant to be ready to flower.

Day 61

Cut the lights on your plants to 10 hours to trigger and sex the plants.

Day 62

Day 63

Week Ten:

Day/Task

Tip of the Week

Remove any leaves that are yellowing, such as the first leaves the plant grew, and all leaves that point toward the inside of the plant in the first tiers of the branches. This 'Leafing' provides better light for the inside buds, and prevents bugs from moving around as easily.

Day 64

Save all your trimmed material in categories. Fans, secondary's and trim leaves all have different uses.

Day 65

Day 66

Day 67

Day 68

Day 69

Day 70

Week Eleven:

Day/Task

Tip of the Week

Long lower braches may be gently bent down to provide the inside of the plant with better light, and make those lower terminals fatten up.

Day 71

Be gentle and bend SLOWLY!

Day 72

Day 73

Day 74

Day 75

Day 76

Day 77

Week Twelve:

Day/Task

Tip of the Week

It is time to flush the nitrogen out, and give a solid Bloom feeding. 6-20-10 is recommended.

Day 78

Day 79

Day 80

Day 81

Day 82

Day 83

Day 84

Week Thirteen:

Day/Task

Tip of the Week

Rule of thumb: Fertillize slightly on the weak side, and dose upwards if needed.

Day 85

Day 86

Day 87

Day 88

Day 89

Day 90

Day 91

Week Fourteen:

Day/Task

Tip of the Week

Observe pistil production and bud Swelling, and be aware that the plant needs more water as it finishes up. Water well, and make sure the pot leaks a little.

Day 92

Day 93

Day 94

Day 95

Day 96

Day 97

Day 98

Week Fifteen:

Day/Task

Tip of the Week

Try some branch bending on the lower branches to feed them light. Apply bloom fertilizer (6-20-10) to give a little nitrogen and induce flowering.

Day 99

Day 100

Day 101

Day 102

Day 103

Day 104

Day 105

Week Sixteen:

Day/Task

Tip of the Week

Flush to finish, and let the plants yellow so they will taste good! Drop lighting to nine hours of light and fifteen dark to finish the final four weeks.

Day 106

Day 107

Day 108

Day 109

Day 110

Day 111

Day 112

Week Seventeen:

Day/Task

Tip of the Week

Rest and observe the plants, fading color. Clean up.

Day 113

Day 114

Day 115

Day 116

Day 117

Day 118

Day 119

Week Eighteen:

Day/Task

Tip of the Week

Watch for hooked or crispy leaf tips and curving of the fan leaves, this indicates the need to flush.

Day 120

Day 121

Day 122

Day 123

Day 124

Day 125

Day 126

Week Nineteen:

Day/Task

Tip of the Week

Remove yellow leaves as they come, they are no longer being used by the plants.

Day 127

Day 128

Day 129

Day 130

Day 131

Day 132

Day 133

Week Twenty:

Day/Task

Tip of the Week

Start reading over the curing section again, and prep your drying area. Clean jars for curing and storage.

Day 134

Day 135

Day 136

Day 137

Day 138

Day 139

Day 140

Week Twenty-One:

Day/Task

Tip of the Week

If the pistils are still flushing, give it more flowering time until pistils die and the buds swell up.

Day 141

Day 142

Day 143

Day 144

Day 145

Day 146

Day 147

Grandaddy Purp

Marijuana Saved My Life, and Continues to Help to This Day

I served 2 years in the active duty Army as mechanized infantry in Germany from 1987 to 1999. After the two years were over, I returned to Germany as a civilian and married my wife of 25 years. When the Berlin wall fell we were laid off so we came to the USA. In 1995, I enlisted into the Kentucky National Guard and was trained as a Tank Mechanic.

After 6 years as a tank mechanic I received my honorable discharge in 2001. I then reenlisted into the Kentucky National Guard in 2003 as a machinist. During this assignment I was retrained as a Line Haul Truck driver and deployed to Iraq. The deployment was for the year 2005 or OIF3 (Operation Iraqi Freedom 3). We only drove the Line Hauls for 4 months in Iraq till they changed our trucks out with gun truck escort trucks. I received all the usual medals including a Combat Action Badge for serving in direct combat on multiple occasions.

Things were quiet when we first arrived in Iraq. That was a good thing too since we were not given the up armored trucks as we were promised. After about 3 months, things got tough. Attacks on the convoys increased heavily but we still were driving trucks that were made in the 60's and 70's and had no armor aside from a quarter inch steel plate welded to the doors to protect from gunfire. These plates did nothing to stop IED's (Improvised Explosive Devices). It wasn't until after a fatality from combat and a letter written home to a Kentucky newspaper that we were actually given the up armored trucks. With the new trucks our mission changed from transporting supplies and ammo to gun truck escort.

I was sent home medically somewhere in month 10. I had injured my neck and the doctor said that I could no longer wear the mandatory body armor that we wore. Without my armor I was not very useful in a combat zone. Although the problem of degenerated discs is not uncommon, it still gives me chronic pain that I feel to this day.

It wasn't until I returned home that I realized I was having serious PTSD (Post Traumatic Stress Disorder) issues. Panic attacks, constant feelings of not being safe, and problems with personal security were some of my symptoms. I was apparently difficult to deal with during this time. My wife and kids knew I needed help. I didn't know that Marijuana helped with any of these things.

I suppose I have to be honest I have to say I was an alcoholic before I went to Iraq but it wasn't until I returned that things got way out of control. I was drinking from the time I woke up till the time I went to bed. I was experiencing PTSD symptoms for the first time as well and I thought the answer was in a bottle. It wasn't until I was drinking a fifth of bourbon a day and still going to get beer that I realized how out of control things had gotten. But realizing it wasn't enough to make me quit so I kept drinking every single day.

I had a nagging pain in my stomach one night that wouldn't let me sleep and having been diagnosed with acid reflux, I thought that this was nothing more than a flare up, but I went to the emergency room anyway. They took blood and I waited for what seemed like forever before they came back and told me that they had never seen test results so out of tolerance. Apparently my blood even messed up the machines that they were using to run the test.

I had what they called a "pseudo cyst" in my pancreas. This is something that is caused and aggravated by alcohol abuse. This condition can easily be fatal if the patient continues to drink. After I went home and got some clothes, they admitted me to the hospital. That stay was about a week. When I say "that stay" I am sure you realize that I didn't quit drinking and had multiple stays in the hospital.

I had smoked marijuana in the past and was getting desperate after my third stay in the hospital, so I decided to try smoking again. The doctors had already told me that I was going to die if I didn't quit drinking so I knew my options were limited. This was difficult because alcoholism runs in my family and killed both my parents. So alcoholism was in my personality from watching my parents while growing up. Some will say its genetic as well. To my relief I noticed that I didn't crave a drink while I was smoking marijuana. I was able to put the drinking habit aside and start new healthy habits. I have now been alcohol free for 6 years. Getting the drinking under control was what I wanted but I also noticed that it helped with the symptoms of PTSD. I still have to take medication from the VA for my PTSD but I am hoping that will end as well once I move to a cannabis friendly state and can grow my own.

For those that think marijuana is for losers, I earned my associates in construction (associate in applied science) while smoking Marijuana and am working toward a bachelor in horticulture now. I don't smoke when I go to school or study and this seems to work well for me. I am not saying that this would work for everyone but to call all marijuana users losers is inaccurate.

Many will say that I substituted alcohol with marijuana. Perhaps I did but I say to them "I am not going to die now." My pancreatitis has been in dormant so to speak for a several years now. I think the damage is there but it's healing and no longer causing me problems. My doctor from the VA has referred to me on multiple occasions as a success story. That coming from the person who has treated me for years means a lot. I am not sure if marijuana has anything to do with it but my doctor has at one time diagnosed me with high blood pressure and type two diabetes, both of those issues are gone now.

My life is good now. My wife and I rarely disagree and we never fight anymore. My panic attacks still happen but they occur less often. My depression is gone. The pain in my neck is manageable. I haven't drunk alcohol in 6 or 7 years and I just passed my one year anniversary for no cigarettes. I cannot say how marijuana does what it does but one thing is clear, it works for me.

To me it's not a matter of if it should be legal or not. Quite simply, I owe marijuana my life. I also owe the ability to deal with life with PTSD to marijuana. Without Marijuana I wouldn't be alive.

— Bill Martin

Jenn's Story
Freedom from Migraines

I began using cannabis in 2011, seeking relief from several medical conditions. The primary disease I was trying to get relief from was migraines. I had been suffering from migraines on an almost daily basis for the past 3 years. When a migraine kicked in, all I could do was lie in a dark, quiet room with ice packs strapped to my forehead and the back of my neck, take high dose Naproxen, and hope that I would sleep until the migraine abated. Sometimes the migraines would be so severe; I had to go to the emergency room at the hospital for intravenous medications, and would have to stay there for several hours at a time.

The migraines were caused partly by genetics (there is a history of migraines in my family) and the degenerative disc disease in my cervical spine. I had osteophytes on 3 discs, bulging discs, and narrowing of the spinal canal.

My quality of life was not good. I was on disability due to the migraines and severe Complex Post Traumatic Stress Disorder (CPTSD). I had been attending university part time since 2010, and had to miss an average of one day per week due to the migraines. I was not able to make plans for the future, even if it was only a couple of days in advance, because I never knew if I was going to be sick with a migraine.

I was very scared to use cannabis medically, due to a history of drug and alcohol addiction. I got "clean and sober" in 2007, and it had been drummed into my head that cannabis is a drug and using it is actively discouraged in the NA and AA communities. I was afraid that if I started using cannabis, it would negatively affect my sobriety.

The alternative though was to continue taking the plethora of psychiatric medications and high dose nonsteroidal anti-inflammatory drugs (nsaids) I had been prescribed, which have been linked to increased risk of heart attacks, heart failure and strokes, in addition to kidney and liver problems.

I researched the various ways to take cannabis aside from smoking it. I decided to try eating cannabis infused olive oil, and to smoke it. The first few times I used it, I noticed that I felt anxious, and had racing thoughts. Practicing mindfulness when this happened helped quite a bit; I drank water and herbal tea, got up and stretched, did some housework, and reminded myself to breathe. Usually within an hour, the anxious feeling subsided, and I was able to sit and watch a movie or read a book.

In the first month of using cannabis, there wasn't a huge decrease in the migraines, but I did notice that I was sleeping better than I had in years. Two of the main symptoms of CPTSD are insomnia and nightmares. I noticed that I was falling asleep easier and staying asleep for longer, which meant that I was actually getting REM sleep, for the first time in a very long time. At this point, I started to consider not taking some of the psychiatric drugs I had been prescribed for the past six years.

I began increasing the amount of cannabis infused olive oil I was taking. I went from a quarter teaspoon in the morning and evening to a half teaspoon in the morning and afternoon, and almost a full teaspoon at night, an hour before bedtime.

The changes I noticed encouraged me to start withdrawing from most of the pharmaceutical drugs I was taking (Topiramate, Trazodone, Quetiapine, Effexor XR). I did not stop these all at once. The first one I stopped taking was Trazodone. Immediately I noticed that I wasn't needing to sleep for 10 hours every night, there was an increase in my energy, and I didn't wake up feeling like I was trying to move through molasses and hung over.

The next drug I discontinued was Topiramate. This had been prescribed to me for off label use, because I was very concerned about the weight I had gained since I started taking the Quetiapine and Effexor. The irony of how many severe migraines I had while taking Topiramate is not lost on me (it is often prescribed off label for migraines; it's intended use is for seizure disorders and epilepsy). Being on Topiramate was incredibly hard due to the side effects. The one I had the most issue with was a huge decrease in my word retrieval ability. I think being in university and most of my classes being seminar style where we were all expected to talk and having to write essays compounded the problem.

I noticed that my appetite had also changed. The intensity of the cravings for sugar and high carbohydrate foods lessened considerably. Combined with having energy, and thinking more clearly, I was able to start cooking for myself on a regular basis, and had an actual desire to go out for walks.

The next drug that I stopped taking was quetiapine. I think it was the hardest withdrawal I have ever experienced. It would not have been possible without cannabis. I increased the amount of infused olive oil to a full teaspoon three times per day, as well as included medibles (cannabis infused edibles, such as cookies and chocolate), and I continued to smoke dried cannabis flowers. The cannabis allowed me to sleep, which was the most important part of coming off that terrible pharmaceutical.

The side effects of Seroquel (quetiapine) seem endless. Suicidal thoughts, dizziness, confusion, high blood sugar, diabetes, uncontrollable jerking movements of the arms and legs, weight gain, sweating, flu like symptoms, just to name a few.

It was around this time that I learned about vaporizers and cannabis. I bought a table-top vaporizer, and was astonished at the difference in the effects of the cannabis compared to smoking it. I liked that I didn't have to worry about the smell while smoking cannabis, or that it would linger on my clothing.

One of the most interesting benefits of using cannabis was the change in my immune system and lungs. Growing up, I was prone to developing lung infections, pneumonia, and bronchitis. I can't think of a winter that I did not get sick and a horrible hacking cough that was so intense I often threw up lingered until late spring. The first year I was using cannabis, I got the flu, and developed a cough that required pharmaceutical medication, but since then, I rarely get sick with a cold or flu, and I haven't had to use inhalers.

The daily migraines I suffered from have become once or twice a month occurrences that I'm able to manage with cannabis, magnesium, ice packs, and a low dose muscle relaxant. If it's a particularly intense migraine, I will take a naproxen, and that is usually enough to stop it from progressing to a full blown migraine (with vomiting and which requires a trip to the ER).

I am now nine months off Effexor XR. My physician told me that I would have to take it for the rest of my life, due to the severity of the withdrawal symptoms I experienced if I was late taking my daily dose of it. I have been using cannabis infused coconut oil instead of the olive oil for four years now. I increased my dose to the equivalent of three tablespoons per day (one and a half in the morning then again at night), then weaned myself off the high dose Effexor XR. The first couple weeks being off Effexor XR were not easy, but it would have been impossible without cannabis.

For the first time in countless years, I'm making plans for several months into the future. I've completed courses and earned excellent grades, which has helped me to grow my small business. I feel better mentally, emotionally, and physically than I have since I was a kid. I look forward to participating in physical activities such as swimming and hiking, and don't fear being incapacitated for days afterwards. I had the first joint in my left big toe surgically removed and fused, and only had to take pharmaceutical opiates for four days; the surgeon had prescribed them for ten days! My goal over the next eighteen months is to discontinue the last prescription antidepressant I am on: Wellbutrin (bupoprion), and to get off federal disability.

I have cannabis to thank for giving me back my life.

— Jenn Hauta

Mark's Story: Struggle with Pain Killers

Back in 2003 I was experiencing severe lower back pain. I disregarded it and continued working hoping it would eventually go away. I was working in Oxford Ohio at the time and was driving to work when out of nowhere something in my spinal cord felt as if it ruptured. The pain was so intense I nearly passed out behind the wheel. I was able to pull over off to the side of the road into a gas station. I exited my vehicle and walked around the lot stretching hoping the pain would subside. I eventually proceeded back towards the job site and after a few miles again the pain hit me. I pulled over again in tears, debating on just going back home but at this point I was closer to work than home.

So again I continued my drive, the pain so intense I was actually experiencing fear at that point. I had no idea what was going on. I got to work late and the pain was so horrific at this point I remained in my car. After 20 minutes or so the job foreman walked over asking if I was working or not? I was in tears at this point and he asks what's wrong. I explained something's wrong with my spine. He told me to take my time and start when I was ready. I must have sat there in my vehicle for what seemed like hours but wasn't, when you're in physical pain time seems to stand still. I ended up going home and to the hospital. I was diagnosed with degenerative Disk disease with 2 herniated disk in my L-4 and l-5 lumbar.

My family doctor gave me some mild pain killers and sent me to see a neurosurgeon. I was 29 at the time, and the Doctor told me I had damage consistent with someone in their 60's. He told me that I was to young for surgery and said to find a pain management doctor. Unhappy with his diagnosis I found another neurosurgeon who had me take an MRI scan. Within a week he insisted I needed surgery.

Before I continue I want you to know the type of person I was. I was extremely active in my life. From a young age I was in sports and shortly after high school met a woman who I married and started a family with. We were independent and everything we obtained we did together, in 94 we had our first child and our second in 95. It was in 93 shortly before we found out we were having a baby that I was offered a Job at Proctor & Gamble thru a friend of my mother's doing graphic design for their products. Part of obtaining the job I was told I had to enroll in college, I felt this would be an excellent opportunity for my wife and I but fate had something else in store because before I could enroll my wife and I found out our first child was coming. I explained my situation and how I needed to keep working for insurance and to provide a home for my wife.

So my education was put on hold, my job opportunity ended because I had to choose work over education and we only had each other. I didn't let that stop me, my company I worked for had other divisions so I applied to become and transfer to the Electrical department. They paid for my education and it seemed our family was going to be ok after all. That is until my injury occurred. In the beginning I was being prescribed 90 mg of OxyContin twice a day. Up until that point in my life I didn't even like taking aspirin.

My neurosurgeon sent me to another doctor, who convinced me that epidural steroid injections might help in alleviating the pain. After dozens of injections I was getting no relief. The pain medication was causing physical and mental problems. I lost nearly 50 pounds in a few months from a loss of appetite. My personality had changed, I was constantly angry, depressed and it was destroying my life. The medications was masking the pain, I had smoked Marijuana when I was younger but had stopped because of my job performing drug test. So a friend stopped by and smoked with me, the affects seemed to instantly change my pain levels, my loss of appetite were subsiding. I ended up further hurting something and went to the hospital, they had me do a urine screen and on my next visit with my doctor at that time informed me I had Cannabis in my system, I explained why and he then accused me of being a dope fiend.

I was not only offended but furious. I yelled at him asking him if that test showed I was abusing my medication, I then went on telling him why I smoked that I wasn't denying I used Cannabis. That's when he pushed me into finding another neurosurgeon who I mentioned earlier gave me an MRI. Upon seeing the results he insisted and arranged for immediate surgery, within a week my first operation was performed, 2 titanium rods held in place by 8 screws. Afterwards, I was sent to another pain management doctor. A year after my first surgery I was given another MRI due to increased pain, which showed the top two screws had broken off at the heads and resulted in my second surgery. The screw heads removed but the parts threaded into my spine left there. Shorter rods were installed with 6 new screws holding them into place.

My life had changed dramatically; I was no longer the man I was. The pain killers only helped to an extent, and my wife gave up on our marriage. My depression from the medication only worsened. Every aspect of my life was falling apart, my job, my family everything that was my meaning in life I was losing. My surgeon then referred my current pain management doctor. He explained that pain medication was something I would have to take for the rest of my life. I explained how it affected me and he explained that finding the correct dosage and combination of medication would help me live a somewhat normal life again.

It took us months in doing so and although the pain was tolerable my mental state was deteriorating. My organs felt like they were breaking down. I continued smoking cannabis so I could maintain an appetite and relieve my depression. I cannot honestly say it was relieving my pain because of the amount of pain medication I was being prescribed. At the time I was on 2 different pain medications. And various other ones...I was taking 2 - 200 mg of MsContin and 10 - 30 mg tablets of oxycodone. 6- 600 mg of Gabapenten 4 times a day, 5 - 25 mg tablets of Topomax, and 8 - 1 mg tablets of Klonipin. I continued taking this for years until the federal government and the state governors changed a law in Ohio and Kentucky that limited what medications my doctor was allowed to prescribe, which by extension limited the amount a patient can take.

In a matter of months he cut every patients medication to levels approved by the federal government... we all know our bodies are all different, that what can work for one person may not suffice for another. I constantly informed my doctor that my pain levels were again unbearable, turning my somewhat life I had again back to the point where I was before. He said its out of his hands and must comply to the law. So I began smoking again more frequently to help control my pain levels, and in doing so I failed my first drug test.

My doctor stated that his position on cannabis is that it's bad and evil. I explained my reasons yet was told I was wrong, and that if I wish to continue seeing him I would have to see a psychologist. Since this law has passed my medication has been cut back to eight 10 mg tablets of oxycodone per day. I take Topomax which is actually seizure medication for my nerve pain.

Due to monthly and random monthly drug test I can only use cannabis for a day or two after my test so I do not risk being kicked off of my medications altogether. Many people who I tell how much I use to take wondered how I could even function.

But what people fail to realize that when you are suffering in constant never ending pain, the pain medication doesn't affect you as it once did.

I have reverted back to spending the majority of my days in bed. It ruined my marriage, my wife divorced me, and my family is gone. Cannabis has been the only alternative that has ever truly helped me without causing more harm to my body and mind. Each month I eagerly wait to take my drug test so for a few days I can use something that actually helps relieve my pain, and my depression. I'm so tired of hurting all of the time. Not having a normal life, being apart from my wife and kids. Those who suffer as I do know what I mean, many of them end up doing what crosses my mind daily.

Cannabis can and does help me, but these laws and the greed of pharmaceutical companies and doctors themselves who are rewarded for pushing their deadly drugs prevent people from having the opportunity to use this miracle plant that is far safer and more effective than the synthetic drugs they profit from.

I don't have the money to move to a state that allows its use medically, even if my state does legalize it , I still cannot afford to purchase it which leaves me only one alternative and that's to grow it myself, but as a part of its legalization here they plan on only allowing a certain number of people with farms the right to grow and supply dispensaries making it a monopoly that they control for one purpose and that's to profit from the people, insurance companies will not cover this -plant.

I hate taking these pain killers, they barely reduce the pain and without proper seeds I cannot supply my own medication, I cannot risk being kicked off what medication I currently take so I must continue to live in pain daily, miserable without hope like so many others.

The sad part is that I have the knowledge, I have the skills, and I have the equipment but not the strains to get started. If I did I would have already been creating my own medication so I wouldn't have to resort to the poison that I'm being forced to take by a government who profits from those like me.

This is my story, like that of so many others many whose lives are far worse than mine. Marijuana is a gift a blessing for people who live in constant never ending pain and we are being tortured over the selfish greed of those who care more about money than other people's lives.

— Mark Fitzpatrick

A Happy Dog's Life

There seems to be much more media attention when it comes to the medical side of cannabis related to us humans than there is for our furry love ones. I'm writing this so I can share my personal experience with the reader. Throughout my life I have had many pets, both cat and dogs.

Dealing with the hardships of pet ownership is not always an easy one. As a young boy I buried a lot of pets that were hit by speeding vehicles. Others were lost for various reasons including things like parvovirus, rabies and even cancer. I always felt so helpless as a boy when it came to the things I could do for them. Most of the time is was all we could do just making them comfortable and staying by their side until the end.

As a teen I discovered cannabis for myself the way many teenagers did, it didn't take me long to realize the personal benefits I was receiving just by smoking it. It wasn't until years later when I learned that it could be concentrated into even more spectacular healing medicine. In the state of Michigan where I live things changed in 2008 when cannabis became legal for medical use (for people) for the very first time since the prohibition of Marijuana in 1937.

I was delighted to be one of the first to be a part of the program and it really spawned a new interest in cannabis for me. Having the illegality of cannabis consumption and cultivation hanging over our heads for decades made it very difficult to learn much of anything in the way of what the cannabis plant can do for us.

Since 2008 I have spent many hours researching, experimenting, growing and using cannabis in its many forms. As the information on how cannabis oil was being used to cure cancer (for people) became available I decided to make my own, it started with the idea I would use it to treat myself. No, I don't have cancer. I have a rare bleeding disorder that's called Hemophilia but that's another story.

In the last few years I have had to move around a bit and didn't always have the chance to grow, instead relying on the medical dispensaries that had begun to pop up but recently that changed. I know grow again for myself and in the process begun to make cannabis oil once again. Now living with my first love (from Jr. High) I came to have a preloaded family of pets. There are two cats, two dogs, two old and two not so old.

They immediately took a liking to me and me to them, even as I constructed the new growing environment they showed interest in what was going on, they would come upstairs and watch. Many discussions between me and my sweetheart as well as my own personal observations were enough of an incentive for me to start treating my new found family.

Emmalee is our oldest dog; she is almost 14 years old now. She has a list of aliments as long as my arm including fatty tumors both internal and external, she has severe arthritis and wasn't able to do things like get on the couch or bed. We had even gone so far as to buy her some steps so she could get up without having to jump. She never did use them. I started her on a 5% - 6% solution of cannabis infused coconut oil. I would give her a dose (.25g) in the morning after she came inside and one at night after the last time she came in for the evening.

The healing effects were almost immediate. Remember this is an animal that has difficulty standing up after she has been lying down and had trouble sleeping due to the level of pain and discomfort she suffers from. After that first morning dose she was already sleeping better, she tended to snore quite loudly and even her breathing had been labored.

After the first day taking the medicine, she made her first attempt at getting on the couch, and even with the stairs still sitting there she made the jump without fail. It was amazing to see the sudden turnaround in her behavior, in a matter of just a few days she had started behaving like a much younger dog. She started being the first one at the door to greet us when we would get home, sometime running out past us then back in before we could both get through the door.

Emmalee likes to walk the perimeter of our yard. Sometimes she would be all the way in the back (about a three quarters of an acre) and normally in the evening we would call them to come in. This would be a long drawn out process of calling and calling because she was so tired getting out that far. She could only take a few steps before having to stop to rest, and then a few more and so on till she would finally get there. Our younger dog Lilly would stand outside the back door and wait for her. Now, whenever Emmalee is called, she can move just as fast as her younger counter part.

I can't tell you how happy it makes me to see her so active. When she came into my life she was very lethargic and stiff and spent most of her time on the floor. I would be happy and totally satisfied if this was the only way it helped, but it isn't. Her eating habits immediately began to improve, and her coat became shinier. Even her breathing was steadier when she slept, and the snoring is all but gone.

As I have mentioned before she has multiple fatty tumors, some lay just under the skin others deeper. It wasn't right away that I noticed but after a few months of the infused coconut oil treatment my girl and I started to notice that one of the tumors near the elbow on her front left arm (one of the largest on the surface) had started to shrink in size.

It was at this point where we decided to give her hands on rubdowns every week thereabouts so we could see if any of the others might be doing the same thing. We started increasing her dosage (.5g twice a day) about a week ago and she is handling it with flying colors. Just a few days ago she ran the full length of the yard to greet my girl as she got home from work, we both stood there looking at each other in amazement.

I have to admit there was a few times where a dose or two was missed, not on purpose mind you but life schedules can be difficult at times. The general observation that we made after about 24 hours without her medication was that Emmalee's activity level had decreased. She had stopped doing little things, like not playing with her stuff animals or fluffing up her blankets and doing her puppy like kneading of them.

We do our best to make sure it doesn't happen and make sure we have a travelling supply on hand for vacationing. This is an ongoing treatment regimen that she will be on as long as she lives, and we are convinced that we've improved the quality of her life and in all reality have added many more years too. She continues to amaze us every day.

— Van M. Bigelow

My Inspirations

I was deeply affected when my mother, Mary Boughen passed away after a lengthy illness, suffering multiple cancers, several radical surgeries, extensive radiation, chemotherapy drugs and then herbal therapies, none of which cured her, and most of which (excluding Chinese Herbal Therapy, which was a great comfort) were directly responsible for shortening her very valuable life as a mother, wife, and inspiration to those who knew her. Cannabis was not a part of her cancer fighting regimen, so I cannot say whether it would have saved her life. I only know that radiation, chemotherapy and pharmaceuticals shortened it.

My journey of Cannabis discovery began the year after she passed on, in the spring of 1998. That year I began to study the Cannabis plant in earnest, reading everything I could on the subject. Family response to my studies was quizzical. Their attitude was more derisive than supportive, more opinion than fact, and much less compassion than understanding. Like the rest, they were hoodwinked by the media and the patter of the snake-oil salesmen selling drugs on television. It didn't matter to me. I determined to find out the true facts, because certain lies had been told, and this to me was cause enough for suspicion about some of the other so-called "facts" about Cannabis that the mainstream media was spouting.

Imagine my waning surprise as I learned that every single negative thing that has ever been said about Cannabis was an outright fabrication or simply a filthy lie based on hate or racism. Even worse, the allegations being made were being supported by junk science, flawed and fudged or simply made up data which is being produced by respected laboratory firms with famous names and international reputations, with trillions in sales worldwide. It seemed to me that patents in need were at the mercy of these organizations, whose only motivation was to profit from the sick and dying.

Over the course of my experiences I know many patients who arrived at the Cannabis treatment option on deaths door and survived, while others come too late or have medical complications, and then even Cannabis cannot save their lives. I already knew Cannabis when cancer came into my body in 2012, and had been studying it fourteen years by that time, so I chose what seemed natural to me. Although I couldn't be sure it would work at the time, nor could I be sure of the drugs and chemo. I was certain that the powerful drugs that were normally prescribed were not the answer I was looking for. A non-toxic alternative was what I wanted. Everything I had learned up until then convinced me that Cannabis was appropriate and worthy of my trust.

In May of 2012 after a blood test, I was diagnosed with prostate Cancer with a PSA of nearly seven. The Oncologist seemed competent, but rather annoyed at my reluctance to accept the therapy she was offering me, which was radioactive seed therapy. This is the implantation of a small radioactive particle or particles near the prostate, which is designed to irradiate the area, thereby theoretically destroying the cancer. This seemed (and still does) like a grossly disproportionate and highly unreasonable response to me, knowing as I do the scientific fact that quite simply put, "radiation is toxic to living tissue.", a thought which terrified me as I realized that the notion was tantamount to a death sentence, or even an attempt at murder for profit.

This radioactive seed therapy was never a viable option in my mind. In a split second I decided that I was going to try a Cannabis oil treatment regimen despite the doctor's insistence that I believed in hokum, and could die without her prescribed treatment. No, I would be my own guinea pig and take a leap of faith in the science behind the endocannabinoid system, for if I believed that cannabis would save my life, I had better prove it, if not for others, then at least for myself. The doctor's solutions made absolutely no sense to me. I deemed the radiation treatment to be harmful based on my own understanding, and the drugs she promised for after-treatment would be permanent, lifetime commitments with serious withdrawal side effects, life threatening symptoms. Deemphasized: If I wanted to I could have some 'pot, for the nausea of the drugs'.

Since I knew that the U.S. government holds the patent on Cannabis as a Cancer treating substance, I believed I held the upper hand in the information department, but still the doctor chided me like a Dutch uncle for performing dangerous experiments on myself. I was shocked by the irony of her apparent lack of understanding, and noted the pot calling the kettle black. None of the treatments she offered had any reasonable chance of "curing" my cancer, but the recovery from treatment was going to be lifelong, and fraught with difficulties brought on by the after-effects of treatment. The Cannabis oil treatment I took is non-toxic and would do no harm at the outset, or require recovery treatment afterwards, and the worst thing they could think of to say was that I 'might be addicted to pot'. (Which I will point out gentle reader, is an absolute lie.)

I was deeply thankful for the declaration of human rights, as well as the Canadian Charter of Rights, because that is what it took to convince the doctor that I had the right (yea, the obligation) to decide on whether any treatment was right, or acceptable to me, and based on my personal structure of belief, no doctor had the right to decide what was best for me and my health, cancer of not. (The right to personal medical choice is presently enshrined in the Canadian Charter of Rights.) Having said that, I am still a little shocked that I had to go to such a great length to protect myself from doctors recommending a toxic radiation treatment and years of addictive pills, side effects and eventual recurrence of cancer somewhere else in my body.

The oncologist was forced to agree that I was in charge of my medical treatment, that all decisions had to be made by me and not her, and any treatment could be accepted or rejected by me as the sovereign owner of my body. The issue had become 'who was in charge of my body', and that is exactly what this entire Cannabis movement is all about. Not legal Cannabis, but freedom of the individual to choose, and the end of government control of the minds and bodies of people.

I did go ahead and take the Cannabis oil treatment, using materials that I legally grew myself and making my own medicine. Frankly, it worked. I knew it would work because the science on the subject and the research into the endocannabinoid system said it would work. I knew literally a dozen well known doctors who said that Cannabis was the cure for cancer, stating their professional reputations that it was true. I'd read a plethora of articles on the endocannabinoid system by eminent scientists, from hundreds of sources, so my information was corroborated from many viewpoints, practices and disciplines.

I cured my own cancer, and went on with my life with no ill after-effects. As a result, I now deliberately go out and tell others about it and encourage them to do the same, and that it is safe rather than dangerous, and that the status quo and the mainstream media is lying.

I cured my own cancer and not a word was said about it, not in the doctor's office or at the Canadian Cancer Society, and hoodwinked people still believe that the cure is beyond us and pour billions into the Ponzi-scheme organizations that feed the lies and budgets of the pharmaceutical companies who feed on death.

The oncologist dropped any interest in my case, she never followed up with me, and to this day I have never heard a single word from the Canadian Cancer Society. The collusion between the doctor's office and the drug company left me with no legal choices, with no options but suffering and murder. They shut the door, sent me home to die with no hope, and I had no choice but to save my own life.

Our legal system is now designed to shelter the powerful from the many, but it won't always be so. Today's immutable and stiff laws must eventually be replaced with flexible justice, which will naturally make for a lasting peace.

Where a compassionate law was allowed, I can assure you I would charge doctors and drug-companies with attempted murder by medical means, and pursue them to the ends of the earth on charges of corruption, profiteering, money laundering, treason, and crimes against humanity. For, experimenting on the unfortunate has been the realm of the privateers, and not the healers.

— Daniel Boughen

Webliography

Video links:

Dr. Robert Melamede

youtube.com/watch?v=b0cSg5CW6PQ

Dr Philip Lavesque

veoh.com/watch/v475236Xmth2jwa?h1=The+Original+%22Dr.+Phil%22!++Dr.+Phillip+Levesque!

Dr Lester Grinspoon

youtube.com/watch?v=8CiqXOTRIL4

Gwen Olson Ex Pharmaceutical Rep: youtube.com/watch?v=UIm8fHxqUAM&feature=player_embedded

Captitate Trichomes: youtube.com/watch?
v=Y_jmVOIQrgg&feature=related

The girl who silenced the world for 5 minutes

youtube.com/watch?v=4EWMUzsGjPM

DrugLibrary Links:

druglibrary.org/Schaffer/library/mj_overdose.htm
druglibrary.org/schaffer/hemp/medical/can-babies.htm

Assorted links:

Ganja Breaks: suitsusall.org/socialeconomics.aspx
LD50 rating of Cannabis: druglibrary.org/Schaffer/library/mj_overdose.htm

Famous Smokers: friendsofcannabis.com/directory/
420magazine.com/forums/celebrity-tokers/87813-200-celebrities-famous-people-who-smoke-pot.html
12–1 (Gas Lantern Routine) cannabisni.com/growingtips-and-advice/1899-grow-bigger-and-better-saving-30-50-percenton-your-energy-cost

Cannabinoid Receptors: en.wikipedia.org/wiki/Cannabinoid
HowsItGoinEh Community : howsitgoineh.com/
Paul V. Nelson book Greenhouse Management 12-1 Short Light Duration

Reports that show the war on drugs has failed:
idpc.net/publications/failure-regime-selected-publications

Reports that show alternative approaches of decriminalization and regulation are working:
idpc.net/publications/alternative-strategies-selected-publications

General report on drug law reform in practice:
tni.org/report/legislative-innovation-drug-policy

The Global Commission on Drug Policy that will call on the UN to end the war on drugs
globalcommissionondrugs.org/Documents.aspx

Drug War by the Numbers
drugpolicy.org/facts/drug-war-numbers

Final Report of the Latin American Commission on Drugs & Democracy
drogasedemocracia.org/English/Destaques.asp?IdRegistro=8

General report on drug law reform in practice:
tni.org/report/legislative-innovation-drug-policy

Kirk Tousaw Lawyer
whyprohibition.ca/category/tags/kirk-tousaw
Dr. William L Courtney:
youtube.com/watch?feature=player_embedded&v=qgEP9FdIzT8#!

Wikipedia Links for AGOP:

en.wikipedia.org/wiki/Arnold_Schwarzenegger
en.wikipedia.org/wiki/Art_Garfunkel
en.wikipedia.org/wiki/Barack_Obama
en.wikipedia.org/wiki/Benjamin_Franklin
en.wikipedia.org/wiki/Bill_Clinton
en.wikipedia.org/wiki/Bill_Gates
en.wikipedia.org/wiki/Bing_Crosby
en.wikipedia.org/wiki/Bob_Denver
en.wikipedia.org/wiki/Bob_Hope
en.wikipedia.org/wiki/Bob_Marley
en.wikipedia.org/wiki/Bruce_Willis
en.wikipedia.org/wiki/Bruce_Lee
en.wikipedia.org/wiki/Burt_Reynolds
en.wikipedia.org/wiki/Calcium
en.wikipedia.org/wiki/Cannabidiol
en.wikipedia.org/wiki/Cannabinol
en.wikipedia.org/wiki/Cannabis
en.wikipedia.org/wiki/Cannabis_sativa
en.wikipedia.org/wiki/Cannabis_Indica
en.wikipedia.org/wiki/Cannabis#Reproduction
en.wikipedia.org/wiki/Carlos_Santana
en.wikipedia.org/wiki/Charlie_Sheen
en.wikipedia.org/wiki/Compact_fluorescent_lamp
en.wikipedia.org/wiki/Circadian_rhythms
en.wikipedia.org/wiki/Chrissie_Hynde
en.wikipedia.org/wiki/Dawn_Wells
en.wikipedia.org/wiki/DEA
en.wikipedia.org/wiki/Deepwater_Horizon_oil_spill
en.wikipedia.org/wiki/Dennis_Hopper
en.wikipedia.org/wiki/Dopamine
en.wikipedia.org/wiki/Dr_Martin_Luther_King
en.wikipedia.org/wiki/DuPont
en.wikipedia.org/wiki/Electrical_conductivity_meter
en.wikipedia.org/wiki/Eminem
en.wikipedia.org/wiki/Endocannabinoid_system
en.wikipedia.org/wiki/EPA
en.wikipedia.org/wiki/George_Clooney
en.wikipedia.org/wiki/George_W_Bush
en.wikipedia.org/wiki/George_Washington_Carver
en.wikipedia.org/wiki/George_Washington
en.wikipedia.org/wiki/Hemp
en.wikipedia.org/wiki/Highintensity_discharge
en.wikipedia.org/wiki/Howard_Marks
en.wikipedia.org/wiki/Iron
en.wikipedia.org/wiki/Jack_Layton
en.wikipedia.org/wiki/Jack_Nicholson
en.wikipedia.org/wiki/Jane_Fonda
en.wikipedia.org/wiki/Jennifer_Aniston
en.wikipedia.org/wiki/Jennifer_Capriati
en.wikipedia.org/wiki/John_Lennon
en.wikipedia.org/wiki/John_Sinclair_%28poet%29
en.wikipedia.org/wiki/Johnny_Depp
en.wikipedia.org/wiki/Jon_Stewart
en.wikipedia.org/wiki/Kate_Moss
en.wikipedia.org/wiki/Kelsey_Grammar
en.wikipedia.org/wiki/Larry_Hagman
en.wikipedia.org/wiki/Lester_Grinspoon
en.wikipedia.org/wiki/Louis_Armstrong
en.wikipedia.org/wiki/Macaulay_Caulkin
en.wikipedia.org/wiki/Magnesium
en.wikipedia.org/wiki/Manganese
en.wikipedia.org/wiki/Margaret_Mead
en.wikipedia.org/wiki/Metal-halide_lamp
en.wikipedia.org/wiki/Michael_Bloomberg
en.wikipedia.org/wiki/Michael_Phelps
en.wikipedia.org/wiki/Montel_Williams
en.wikipedia.org/wiki/Mycorrhiza
en.wikipedia.org/wiki/Neem_oil
en.wikipedia.org/wiki/Nitrogen
en.wikipedia.org/wiki/NPK_rating
en.wikipedia.org/wiki/Oscar_Wilde
en.wikipedia.org/wiki/Oliver_Stone
en.wikipedia.org/wiki/Peter_Tosh
en.wikipedia.org/wiki/Peter_Sellers
en.wikipedia.org/wiki/Pierre_Elliot_Trudeau
en.wikipedia.org/wiki/PH
en.wikipedia.org/wiki/PH_meter
en.wikipedia.org/wiki/Phosphorous
en.wikipedia.org/wiki/Phyllotaxy
en.wikipedia.org/wiki/Pancho_Villa
en.wikipedia.org/wiki/Potassium
en.wikipedia.org/wiki/Powdery_mildew
en.wikipedia.org/wiki/Ray_Charles
en.wikipedia.org/wiki/Richard_Pryor
en.wikipedia.org/wiki/Robert_Mitchum
en.wikipedia.org/wiki/Rodney_Dangerfield
en.wikipedia.org/wiki/Reefer_Madness
en.wikipedia.org/wiki/Rooting_powder
en.wikipedia.org/wiki/Salvidor_Dali
en.wikipedia.org/wiki/Sir_Winston_Churchill
en.wikipedia.org/wiki/Steven_King
en.wikipedia.org/wiki/Steve_Martin
en.wikipedia.org/wiki/Stephen_Sondheim
en.wikipedia.org/wiki/Ted_Turner
en.wikipedia.org/wiki/THC
en.wikipedia.org/wiki/Timothy_Leary
en.wikipedia.org/wiki/Thalidomide
en.wikipedia.org/wiki/Thomas_Jefferson
en.wikipedia.org/wiki/T5_fluorescent_lamp#T5_tubes
en.wikipedia.org/wiki/Tommy_Chong
en.wikipedia.org/wiki/Total_dissolved_solids
en.wikipedia.org/wiki/Victor_Hugo
en.wikipedia.org/wiki/William_Shakespeare
en.wikipedia.org/wiki/Walter_Benjamin
en.wikipedia.org/wiki/War_on_Drugs
en.wikipedia.org/wiki/
en.wikipedia.org/wiki/Woodie_Guthrie
en.wikipedia.org/wiki/Woody_Harrelson

Personal Acknowledgements

Ted Smith (forward)
Van M. Bigelow (additional photos, testimonial)
Emma Lee (for being a happy dog)
Lisa (Mamakind) Kirkman
Noah Kirkman (testimonial)
Bill and Brigit Martin (testimonial)
Jenn Hauta (testimonial)
Andrew Sargeant (additional photos)
Mark Fitzpatrick (testimonial)
Chris Butts
Kris Millegan
Ed Bishop
and many others, whose encouragement is a beacon, thanks for everything.

ROCKY MOUNTAIN EXTRACTIONS
ROCKY MTN MEDIBLES

The Marijuana Lover's Guide to Gettin' It On
Sex Pot
Sexy Stoner Advice From Cannabis Columnist
MAMAKIND
Available at:
QuickTrading.com
Amazon.com
and at kind retailers near you!

Helping those with incurable illnesses
SINCE 1996
GAYLE QUIN MEDICINAL PRODUCTS
CBC
HIGH QUALITY EDIBLES AND TOPICALS
CLUB BEHIND SMITH EXTRACT DECISION
MEMBERS VAPOUR LOUNGE
VICTORIA CANNABIS BUYERS CLUB
INFO@V-CBC.CA
V-CBC.CA

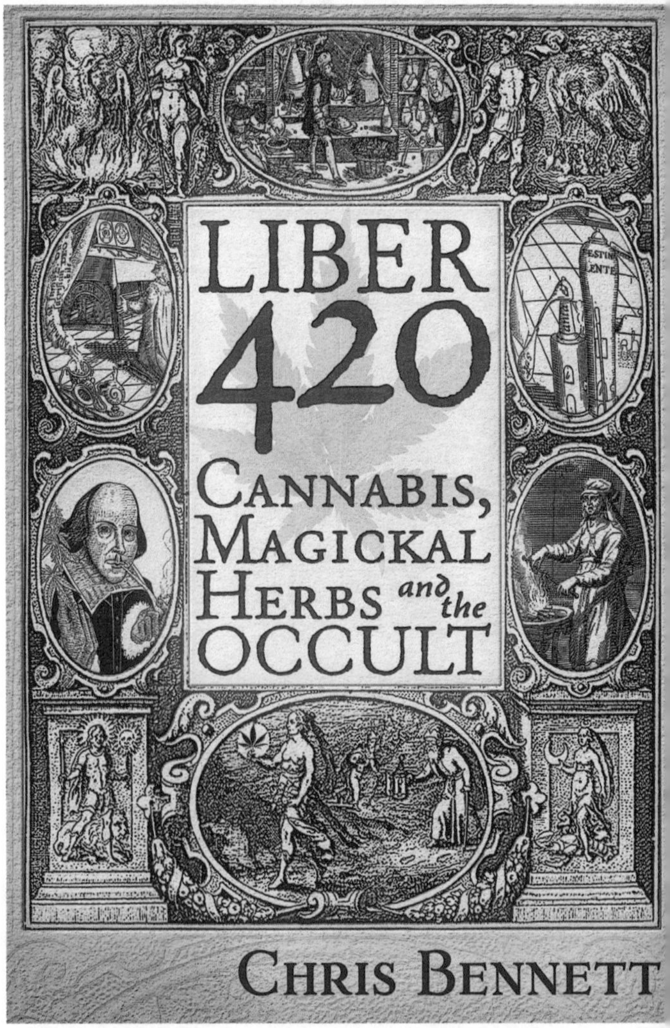
LIBER 420
CANNABIS, MAGICKAL HERBS and the OCCULT
CHRIS BENNETT

Green Bluff
GREENHOUSE
GROWN ON
GREEN BLUFF
greenbluffgreenhouse.com

Lamourie
Public Relations
Professional Media For Canna Companies
We Can Take You Higher
Toronto, Los Angeles, New York
lamouriePR@gmail.com
#GetRepped

dnrack.com
Canna-business
Social Activist
Web-building
and Hosting.
bones@dnrack.com

Medical
Growing
A Garden of Peace
Daniel Boughen
Foreword by Ted Smith
Signed copies @ www.agardenofpeace.com
EXPANDED SECOND EDITION

Daniel's Lemon OG
10 seeds for $75 Free S&H
OG/UK Cheese, Vortex
higedonations@gmail.com

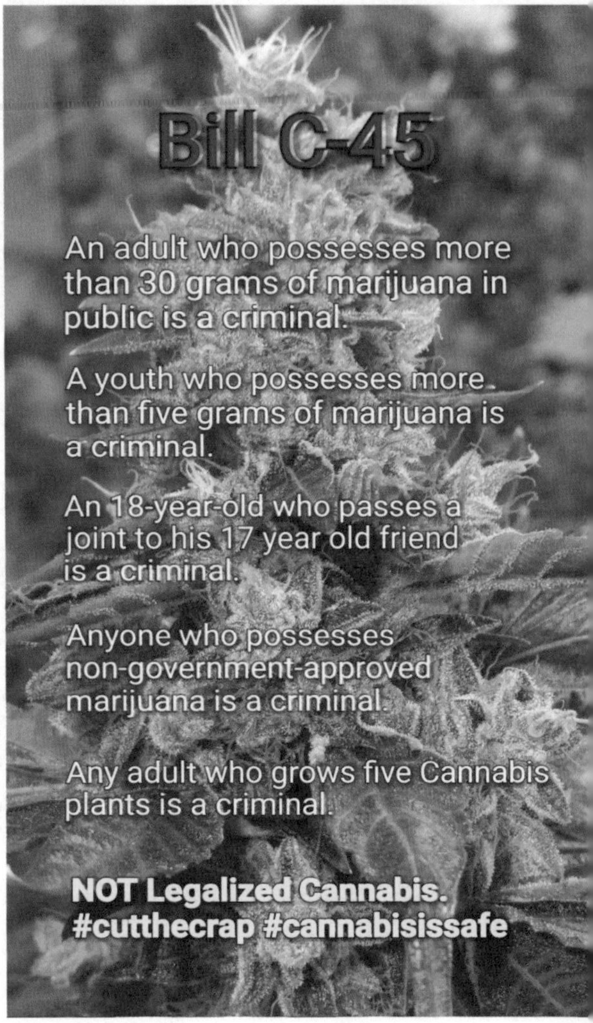
Bill C-45
An adult who possesses more than 30 grams of marijuana in public is a criminal.
A youth who possesses more than five grams of marijuana is a criminal.
An 18-year-old who passes a joint to his 17 year old friend is a criminal.
Anyone who possesses non-government-approved marijuana is a criminal.
Any adult who grows five Cannabis plants is a criminal.
NOT Legalized Cannabis.
#cutthecrap #cannabisissafe

The Cannabis hypocrisy can be summed up like this:
A) "Cannabis is bad for you?."
Answer: For sure! We have doctor's studies suggesting that it MAY cause "so and so".
B) "Cannabis is good for you?"
Answer: Their are no studies. We don't have enough information that it works at all.
It will take time to research.